PREFACE

1. Scope

This publication provides doctrine for planning, preparing, executing, and assessing joint interdiction operations.

2. Purpose

This publication has been prepared under the direction of the Chairman of the Joint Chiefs of Staff. It sets forth joint doctrine to govern the activities and performance of the Armed Forces of the United States in joint operations and provides the doctrinal basis for interagency coordination and for US military involvement in multinational operations. It provides military guidance for the exercise of authority by combatant commanders and other joint force commanders (JFCs) and prescribes joint doctrine for operations, education, and training. It provides military guidance for use by the Armed Forces in preparing their appropriate plans. It is not the intent of this publication to restrict the authority of the JFC from organizing the force and executing the mission in a manner the JFC deems most appropriate to ensure unity of effort in the accomplishment of the overall objective.

3. Application

a. Joint doctrine established in this publication applies to the joint staff, commanders of combatant commands, subunified commands, joint task forces, subordinate components of these commands, and the Services.

b. The guidance in this publication is authoritative; as such, this doctrine will be followed except when, in the judgment of the commander, exceptional circumstances dictate otherwise. If conflicts arise between the contents of this publication and the contents of Service publications, this publication will take precedence unless the Chairman of the Joint Chiefs of Staff, normally in coordination with the other members of the Joint Chiefs of Staff, has provided more current and specific guidance. Commanders of forces operating as part of a multinational (alliance or coalition) military command should follow multinational doctrine and procedures ratified by the United States. For doctrine and procedures not ratified by the United States, commanders should evaluate and follow the multinational command's doctrine and procedures, where applicable and consistent with US law, regulations, and doctrine.

For the Chairman of the Joint Chiefs of Staff:

WILLIAM E. GORTNEY
VADM, USN
Director, Joint Staff

Intentionally Blank

SUMMARY OF CHANGES
REVISION TO JOINT PUBLICATION 3-03
DATED 03 MAY 2007

- **Includes more detailed discussion of interdiction in the maritime domain, to include introducing the terms "air interdiction of maritime targets" and "maritime air support."**

- **Adds discussion about the execution of interdiction in irregular warfare (IW). Specifically examines the role of collateral damage and nonlethal means (such as interdiction operations in cyberspace and military information support operations), and their impact on interdiction operations in an IW or counterinsurgency environment.**

- **Includes increased discussion of interagency support to interdiction operations. Specific topics include a summary of other government agency capabilities, the means to conduct integrated planning with other departments and agencies, and the method to communicate the whole of government plan.**

- **Adds discussion of military interdiction operations in support of law enforcement and homeland defense missions.**

- **Examines legal considerations when conducting interdiction in multiple environments, to include legal bases for maritime interdiction, and legal restrictions on certain interdiction methods and weapons.**

- **Provides greater detail on weapons of mass destruction interdiction.**

- **Provides a more concise description of full spectrum superiority and its relationship to successful interdiction operations.**

- **Refines the description of the use of unmanned aircraft in interdiction operations.**

Intentionally Blank

TABLE OF CONTENTS

GLOSSARY

FIGURE

EXECUTIVE SUMMARY
COMMANDER'S OVERVIEW

- **Presents the Fundamentals of Interdiction**

- **Discusses Joint Interdiction Capabilities**

- **Explains Joint Interdiction Planning, to Include Command Relationships, Integrating Interdiction and Maneuver, and Targeting**

- **Describes Joint Interdiction Execution, to Include Command and Control, Linear and Nonlinear Operations, Coordinating Measures, and Assessment**

Fundamentals of Interdiction

Joint force commanders (JFCs) may employ interdiction operations as a principal means to achieve intended objectives.

Interdiction operations are actions to divert, disrupt, delay, or destroy an enemy's surface capabilities before they can be used effectively against friendly forces, or to otherwise achieve objectives. In support of law enforcement, interdiction includes activities conducted to divert, disrupt, delay, intercept, board, detain, or destroy, under lawful authority, vessels, vehicles, aircraft, people, cargo, and money.

Interdiction in Joint Operations

Joint force commanders (JFCs) integrate and synchronize operations and employ military forces and capabilities, as well as nonmilitary resources, across the range of military operations resulting in greater combat power and operational effectiveness. JFCs arrange symmetrical and asymmetrical actions to take advantage of friendly strengths and enemy vulnerabilities and to preserve freedom of action for future operations. Interdiction can create opportunities for commanders to exploit and should be integrated with other operations of the joint force.

Purpose of Interdiction Operations

The purpose of interdiction operations is to prevent the adversary from using assets at the time and place of his choosing.

Diversion. Interdiction can divert enemy forces or assets from areas where there are critical operational requirements for them.

Disruption. Joint force actions supporting disruption will interrupt or impede enemy or enemy capabilities or systems, upsetting the flow of information, operational tempo, effective interaction, or cohesion of the enemy force or those systems.

Delay. Joint force actions can delay the time of arrival of enemy forces or capabilities or alter the ability of the enemy or adversary to project forces or capabilities.

Destroy. Joint force actions supporting destruction will damage the structure, function, or condition of a target so that it can neither perform as intended nor be restored to a usable condition, rendering it ineffective or useless.

Interdiction Objectives

Interdiction may be planned to create advantages at any level from tactical to strategic with corresponding effects on the enemy and the speed with which interdiction affects frontline enemy forces. Interdiction deep in the enemy's rear area can have broad operational effects; however, deep interdiction may have a delayed effect on land and maritime operations. Interdiction closer to land and maritime forces will be of more immediate operational and tactical concern to maneuver forces. During major operations and campaigns the effects of interdiction are typically more influential when directed against an enemy's ability to command, mass, maneuver, supply, and reinforce available conventional combat forces.

Elements of Effective Interdiction

Effective interdiction operations share a number of common elements, which lead to the attainment of interdiction objectives. The mix of elements in each operation depends on such variables as the nature of the conflict, geographic location, weather, and enemy characteristics. Elements normally required to successfully prosecute interdiction operations are **full spectrum superiority, synchronization with maneuver; sustained and concentrated pressure; accurate, reliable, and timely intelligence; and effective resource planning, positioning, and allocation.**

Joint Interdiction Capabilities

Interdiction-Capable Forces

Interdiction operations can be conducted by all components of the joint force, across the range of military operations employing both lethal and nonlethal means.

Air forces employ such weapons as projectiles, missiles, unguided munitions, precision munitions, land and/or sea mines, electronic warfare systems, and sensors from airborne platforms.

Maritime forces employ assets such as surface combatants, carriers, amphibious shipping, aircraft, helicopters, submarines, landing forces, and special forces, and weapons such as missiles, munitions, torpedoes, and mines, capable of conducting a variety of air, land, and sea operations.

Land forces employ such assets as attack helicopters, missiles, artillery, and those forces capable of conducting conventional airborne, air assault, and amphibious operations.

Special operations forces may support conventional interdiction operations by providing terminal guidance for precision-guided munitions, or may act independently when the use of conventional forces is inappropriate or infeasible.

Other government agencies work with military forces in a "whole of government" approach to interdiction capabilities and forces. Military elements work with our interagency partners (Department of the Treasury, Federal Bureau of Investigation, etc.) to interdict threat finance and foreign fighter streams.

Complementary Operations

Joint interdiction operations are most effective when fully integrated with other air, land, sea, space, information, and special operations of the joint force. In addition to counterair and maneuver, other operations notable for their specialized roles which can complement joint interdiction operations include the following: strategic attack operations;

intelligence, surveillance, and reconnaissance; space operations; information operations; air refueling; and strike coordination and reconnaissance.

Joint Interdiction Planning

Unity of effort, centralized planning, and decentralized execution are key to success in joint and interagency interdiction operations.

The manner in which the JFC plans, organizes, and directs forces affects the responsiveness and versatility of joint interdiction operations. JFCs employ forces to accomplish their objectives; the principal challenge is to combine force capabilities and operations to create effects that support achievement of those objectives. Joint interdiction typically focuses on operational level objectives as delineated in the JFC's operation or campaign plans. It must also support strategic level objectives by working in concert with other efforts to neutralize or destroy the enemy's centers of gravity or other key target systems.

Operations extended in depth, in time as well as space, shape future conditions and can disrupt an opponent's decision cycle.

Interdiction is one manner in which JFCs add depth to operations at the operational level. The intent of deep operations is to bring force to bear on the opponent's entire structure, at the tactical, operational, and strategic depths, in a near simultaneous manner. Although it has usually been the case that interdiction closer to surface forces was designed to affect the battle over a shorter term than actions deeper in the enemy's territory, the most important aspect in planning interdiction operations is the effect desired, which may be measured in time. The JFC should not apply strict geographic boundaries to interdiction, but should plan for its theater/joint operations area (JOA)-wide application.

Command Relationships

It is important to note that joint interdiction can be conducted inside an area of operations (AO) in direct response to JFC tasking, and

JFCs typically conduct joint interdiction operations through component commanders. All elements of the joint force can be called upon to perform interdiction operations. The JFC structures the joint force to ensure that diverse component capabilities, operations, and forces complement each other to achieve the desired results effectively and efficiently. To ensure unity of command and effort of air operations throughout a theater/JOA, the JFC normally delegates the planning and execution of theater/JOA-wide air interdiction operations to the *may not be in support of the AO commander.*

component commander, with the preponderance of air interdiction assets with theater/JOA-wide range and the ability to control them. **The joint force air component commander (JFACC) is normally the supported commander for the JFC's overall air interdiction effort, while land and maritime component commanders are supported commanders for interdiction in their areas of operations (AOs).**

Integrating Interdiction and Maneuver

Maneuver and interdiction could be conducted relatively independent of each other in certain circumstances. However, integrating interdiction and maneuver, as well as their joint fires, enhances the ability for each to more fully contribute to a successful outcome of a campaign or major operation. Interdiction and maneuver are complementary operations that should normally be integrated to create dilemmas for the enemy.

Planning Joint Interdiction

Components may conduct interdiction operations as part of their specific mission in addition to, or in lieu of, supporting the theater/joint operations area-wide interdiction effort. In such situations as these, command and control for the operation is normally conducted according to the component's procedures.

The JFC establishes broad planning objectives and guidance for interdiction of enemy forces as an integral part of a joint campaign or major operation. Subordinate commanders recommend to the JFC how to use their combat power more effectively to this end. With this advice, the JFC sets interdiction priorities, provides targeting guidance, and makes apportionment decisions. The JFACC's air interdiction employment guidance, based on the JFC's air apportionment decision, is used by the joint air operations center for input into the air tasking order. Land and maritime commanders, as supported commanders within their AOs, the land and maritime force commanders are responsible for integrating and synchronizing maneuver, fires, and interdiction within their AOs.

Targeting

During target development, the targeting process must relate specific targets to objectives, desired effects, and accompanying actions. Interdiction should focus on those systems that will result in the greatest payoff and achieve the objectives. The goal for interdiction targeting is to execute a connected series of missions and attacks to achieve the JFC's interdiction objectives.

Dynamic interdiction missions respond to targets that require time sensitive or immediate attention. The same quick-responsive nature of dynamic interdiction that allows it to take advantage of fleeting opportunities can also have a negative impact on individual mission success.

Deliberate interdiction requests allow joint interdiction forces more time to study target imagery and to align attack axes to optimize weapons effects. Detailed study can reduce threat exposure and allow mission planners to optimize the weapon's fusing for maximum effect.

Intelligence, Surveillance, and Reconnaissance Strategy and Planning

Intelligence, surveillance, and reconnaissance forces support interdiction planning through the collection of and collaboration on a broad range of information. Priority intelligence requirements are developed to support interdiction operations. To that end, joint interdiction targets must be identified and then prioritized to facilitate collection management and mission accomplishment.

Interdiction Planning Considerations

The nature of the mission or a target set may determine its suitability for interdiction and what forces and weapon systems should be employed.

Target area environmental considerations include restrictive terrain, time of day, adverse weather, as well as seasonal and temperature effects.

Interdiction operations in urban areas can be problematic and require special considerations during planning. To begin with, collateral damage in cities or towns that have not been evacuated will represent a great risk that must be considered and minimized. Planners and operators should take great care in choosing the correct delivery method, munition, and fusing option when employing fires in an urban environment.

Joint forces operate in accordance with applicable **rules of engagement**, conduct warfare consistent with **international laws** recognized by the US, and operate within **restraints and constraints** specified by their commanders.

Joint forces should be prepared for operations with forces from other nations within the **framework of an alliance or coalition.**

Joint Interdiction Execution

Command and Control of Joint Interdiction Operations

The joint operations center is the focal point for integrating joint operations at the macro level to include interdiction. **Joint interdiction operations require an integrated, flexible, and responsive command and control (C2) structure to process interdiction requirements and a dependable, interoperable, and secure communications architecture to exercise control.**

The **theater air control system (TACS)** is the Air Force component commander's mechanism for controlling component air interdiction assets.

The **Army air-ground system (AAGS)** provides for interface between Army and tactical air support agencies of other Services in the planning, evaluating, processing, and coordinating of air support requirements and operations.

The **Navy tactical air control system (NTACS)** is the principal air control system afloat.

The **Marine air command and control system (MACCS)** consists of various air C2 agencies designed to provide the Marine air-ground task force aviation combat element commander with the ability to monitor, supervise, and influence the application of Marine and supporting air assets.

When all elements of the TACS, AAGS, MACCS, and NTACS integrate, the entire system is labeled the **Theater air-ground system [TAGS].**

Operational Area Geometry and Coordination

JFCs may employ various control and coordinating measures to facilitate effective joint operations. These measures may include establishing boundaries, objectives, coordinating altitudes to deconflict air operations, air defense areas, amphibious objective areas, and submarine operating areas.

Joint interdiction may be conducted in conjunction with friendly forces operating in an AO. In order to integrate joint fires and avoid fratricide, fire support coordination measures (FSCMs) must be established. When air operations are involved, airspace coordinating measures will normally be used along with FSCMs.

Linear and Nonlinear Operations

In linear operations, commanders direct and sustain combat power toward enemy forces in concert with adjacent units. Linear perspective refers primarily to the conduct of operations along lines of operations with identified forward lines of own troops (FLOTs).

In nonlinear operations, forces orient on objectives without geographic reference to adjacent forces. Nonlinear operations emphasize simultaneous operations along multiple lines of operation from selected bases.

Coordinating Measures

There are two important constructs to understand when discussing coordinating measures.

- The **forward boundary** defines a component's outer AO and is the farthest limit of an organization's responsibility.

- The **FLOT** is a line that indicates the most forward positions of friendly forces during linear operations at a specific time.

Fire Support Coordination Measures

Within their AOs, land and naval force commanders employ permissive and restrictive FSCMs. FSCMs are necessary to facilitate the rapid engagement of targets and simultaneously provide safeguards for friendly forces. **Permissive FSCMs facilitate attacks** and include coordinated fire lines, free fire areas, fire support coordination lines (FSCLs), and kill boxes. **Restrictive measures safeguard friendly forces** and include no-fire areas, restrictive fire areas, restrictive fire lines, and airspace coordination areas.

Fire Support Coordination Line

When appropriate, an FSCL will be established and adjusted by appropriate land or amphibious force commanders within their assigned boundaries in consultation with superior, subordinate, supporting, and affected commanders. The purpose of the FSCL is to facilitate the expeditious attack of surface targets of opportunity beyond the coordinating measure. Attacks on surface targets short of the FSCL during the conduct of joint interdiction operations must be controlled by and/or coordinated with the appropriate land or amphibious force commander. Joint interdiction forces attacking targets beyond the FSCL must inform all affected commanders in sufficient time to allow necessary reaction to avoid friendly casualties.

Kill Box

A **kill box** is a three-dimensional area used to facilitate the integration of joint fires. When established, the primary purpose of a kill box is to allow lethal attack against surface targets without further coordination with the establishing commander and without terminal attack control.

Assessment

Commanders continuously assess the operational environment and the progress of operations, and compare them to their initial vision and intent. Joint interdiction operations should include both pre- and post-interdiction target reconnaissance efforts in order to facilitate combat assessment. Information gained from combat assessment provides input for follow-on interdiction efforts.

CONCLUSION

This publication provides doctrine for planning, preparing, executing, and assessing joint interdiction operations.

Intentionally Blank

CHAPTER I
FUNDAMENTALS OF INTERDICTION

"An army can be defeated by one of two main alternative means—not necessarily mutually exclusive: we can strike at the enemy's troops themselves, either by killing them or preventing them from being in the right place at the right time; or we can ruin their fighting efficiency by depriving them of their supplies of food and war material of all kinds on which they depend for existence as a fighting force."

Wing Commander J. C. Slessor
Air Power and Armies, 1936

1. Introduction

This publication provides a basis for the planning, execution, and assessment of interdiction operations. **Interdiction operations are actions to divert, disrupt, delay, or destroy an enemy's surface capabilities before they can be used effectively against friendly forces, or to otherwise achieve objectives. In support of law enforcement, interdiction includes activities conducted to divert, disrupt, delay, intercept, board, detain, or destroy, under lawful authority, vessels, vehicles, aircraft, people, cargo, and money.** Interdiction also can be used to prevent an adversary from achieving a variety of objectives affecting the US populace, economy, or national interests. With regard to military operations in conventional terms, they are conducted at such distance from friendly surface forces that detailed integration of each mission with the fire and maneuver of those forces is not required. **Interdiction operations may support theater/joint operations area (JOA)-wide priorities or component operations.** Doctrine for joint interdiction operations can be applied across the range of military operations. Due to the nature of modern conflict that involves nation states, non-state actors, and other threats to the US, interdiction operations can span from US shores, across the open seas, and into theaters or JOAs. These operations may complement, support, or be supported by maneuver operations. When directed, other government agencies (OGAs) may support joint interdiction operations or conduct their own interdiction activities. Interdiction-capable forces are discussed in Chapter II, "Joint Interdiction Capabilities." Joint force commanders (JFCs) may employ interdiction operations as a principal means to achieve intended objectives.

2. Interdiction in Joint Operations

To fully appreciate the dynamics of interdiction and the role it fulfills in joint campaigns and operations, one first needs to place it in the context of operational design. JFCs integrate and synchronize operations and employ military forces and capabilities, as well as nonmilitary resources, across the range of military operations resulting in greater combat power and operational effectiveness. Further, JFCs seek combinations of forces and actions to achieve concentration in the shortest time possible and with minimal casualties to achieve military objectives. JFCs also gain decisive advantage over the enemy through leverage. Leverage can be achieved in a variety of ways. JFCs arrange symmetrical and asymmetrical actions to take advantage of friendly strengths and enemy vulnerabilities and to preserve freedom of action for future operations.

a. The history of joint operations highlights the enormous lethality of asymmetrical operations and the great operational sensitivity to such threats. Asymmetrical operations are particularly effective when applied against enemy forces not postured for immediate tactical battle but instead operating in more vulnerable aspects—operational deployment and/or movement, extended logistic activity (including rest and refitting), or mobilization and training (including industrial production). Thus, JFCs must aggressively seek opportunities to apply asymmetrical force against an enemy in as vulnerable an aspect as possible—air attacks against enemy ground formations in convoy (e.g., the air and special operations forces [SOF] interdiction operations against German attempts to reinforce its forces in Normandy), naval air attacks against troop transports (e.g., US air attacks against Japanese surface reinforcement of Guadalcanal), and land operations against enemy naval, air, or missile bases (e.g., allied maneuver in Europe in 1944 to reduce German submarine bases and V-1 and V-2 launching sites).

b. Interdiction can create opportunities for commanders to exploit and should be integrated with other operations of the joint force. It can significantly affect the course of a campaign or major operation. However, the use of interdiction must be tailored to the situation and should be closely integrated in the JFC's overall strategy. Interdiction against an enemy with a rigid, top-down command and control (C2) structure differs from the rapid, agile interdiction required against a decentralized, networked terrorist organization or insurgency. Interdiction can be particularly effective when the enemy must rapidly move major forces and their sustaining supplies.

3. Purpose of Interdiction Operations

The purpose of interdiction operations is to prevent the adversary from using assets at the time and place of his choosing. The terms are not mutually exclusive. Actions associated with one desired effect may also support the others. For example, delay can result from disrupting, diverting, or destroying enemy capabilities or targets.

a. **Diversion.** Interdiction can divert enemy forces or assets from areas where there are critical operational requirements for them. Its purpose is to consume resources or capabilities critical to enemy operations in a way that is advantageous to friendly operations. It may divert enemy ground forces to a location more favorable to the JFC or divert enemy naval, engineering, and personnel resources to the tasks of repairing and recovering damaged equipment, facilities, and lines of communications (LOCs). It can draw the attention of enemy forces away from critical friendly operations. These diversions prevent enemy forces and their support resources from being employed for their intended purpose. Diversions can also cause more circuitous routing along LOCs, resulting in delays for the enemy. Diversion may be effective in the interdiction of weapons of mass destruction (WMD) material.

b. **Disruption.** Joint force actions supporting disruption will interrupt or impede enemy or enemy capabilities or systems, upsetting the flow of information, operational tempo, effective interaction, or cohesion of the enemy force or those systems. Interdiction can disrupt the enemy's C2 systems, intelligence collection capability, transportation systems, supply lines, industrial base, and psychological will. Interdiction thus disrupts the movement and routing of the enemy's information, materiel, and forces. Disruption can result from degradation or destruction of these enemy capabilities. Disruption of enemy surface forces can be accomplished in a number of ways. A key task during interdiction planning is analyzing the enemy for critical vulnerabilities that, if attacked, will have a disruptive effect across significant portions of the enemy force.

(1) The enemy's combat operations may be disrupted with attacks on their C2 nodes or key commercial infrastructure components, such as electrical power and transportation, which support and sustain enemy operations. Such attacks may force the enemy to use less capable, less secure backup communications systems that can be more easily exploited by friendly forces. Regimes that possess a rigid, top-down C2 structure can be particularly vulnerable to interdiction.

(2) Interdiction can disrupt by attacking enemy LOCs, forcing the enemy to use less capable transportation modes to communicate and sustain its forces. These disruptive effects can severely affect the tempo of enemy operations and ultimately force the enemy to culminate earlier than anticipated.

(3) Interdiction attacks can also produce a psychological impact which could significantly reduce enemy capabilities and morale. Uncertainty as to whether or not forces, materiel, or supplies will arrive can directly affect enemy commanders, their staffs, and forces.

(4) Disruption can also be achieved through nonlethal means in support of counterterrorism, combating WMD, law enforcement, or national and/or international sanction activities. The purpose of these nonlethal actions is to impede unlawful activities or activities that pose a threat, whether in the context of a conflict with an enemy or in civil support actions. In modern complex operations, the adversary is often neither easily recognized nor a uniformed, armed combatant. In such an environment, activities such as boarding, diverting and seizing, if feasible, are frequently more appropriate than lethal attacks.

c. **Delay.** Joint force actions can delay the time of arrival of enemy forces or capabilities or alter the ability of the enemy or adversary to project forces or capabilities.

(1) When interdiction delays the enemy, friendly forces gain time. What JFCs do to improve their situation in the time gained is critical to any assessment of interdiction's contribution. However, an interdiction plan that focuses on delay and is effectively executed does not guarantee a major impact on operations. For delay to have a major impact, either the enemy must face urgent movement requirements, or the delay must enhance the effect(s) of planned friendly operations.

(2) It is advantageous for friendly forces to pressure their opponent to attempt time-urgent movement. Ideally, if the joint force maintains the initiative the opponent is forced to

make unplanned time-urgent movements, at times and places that maximize their vulnerability to interdiction.

(3) The intent of interdiction may be to lengthen the time during which enemy land or naval forces are at risk of attack. When vehicles mass behind a damaged route segment, or ships are trapped in a harbor because of mines, a more concentrated set of targets and a longer period of exposure results. If there are follow-on strikes, this makes the enemy easier to destroy or render ineffective.

d. **Destroy.** Joint force actions supporting destruction will damage the structure, function, or condition of a target so that it can neither perform as intended nor be restored to a usable condition, rendering it ineffective or useless. The destruction of enemy forces, cargoes, support elements, and resources is the most direct form of interdiction. This level of interdiction may not always require follow up missions or a sustained campaign. Destroying transportation systems is usually not an end in itself, but contributes to the delay, diversion, and disruption of enemy forces and materiel. It may also produce unintended or undesirable effects. It may cause the enemy to mass air defense assets, which may be useful elsewhere, around critical transportation nodes. It may force the enemy to use alternate, less efficient routes or disperse critical assets. The enemy may have to divert engineering resources from other tasks to prepare alternate routes in anticipation of possible attacks. This may be true even when transportation systems remain largely undamaged. However, destruction may also inhibit friendly freedom of action. For example, destruction of key enemy transportation infrastructure in and around land and naval areas of operations (AOs) could hinder subsequent friendly surface operations. Appropriate coordination of interdiction helps to preserve friendly freedom of action. Knowledge of the enemy helps the JFC to anticipate the reactions and consequences of a destruction-oriented interdiction upon all stakeholders — enemies, populace, friends, allies, and sympathizers. Additionally, collateral damage and other unintended effects may influence the commander's decision to use these types of fires in urban areas.

4. Interdiction Objectives

a. The effectiveness of interdiction is dependent on a number of factors to include: the distance between interdiction operations and the location of intended effect; the means and rate of movement (ships, trains, aircraft, trucks); the physical target (forces, cargo/passengers, supplies, fuel, munitions, infrastructure); the level of enemy activity; enemy tactics; and the resilience, adaptability, persistence, and resourcefulness of the enemy or its targeted force or system. Interdiction may be planned to create advantages at any level from tactical to strategic with corresponding effects on the enemy and the speed with which interdiction affects frontline enemy forces. Interdiction deep in the enemy's rear area can have broad operational effects; however, deep interdiction may have a delayed effect on land and maritime operations. Interdiction closer to land and maritime forces will be of more immediate operational and tactical concern to maneuver forces. Thus, JFCs vary the emphasis upon interdiction operations and surface maneuvers, depending on the strategic and operational situation confronting them. During major operations and campaigns the effects of interdiction are typically more influential when directed against an enemy's ability to command, mass, maneuver, supply, and reinforce available conventional combat forces.

Interdiction is more difficult against an enemy that employs a covert force structure, a simple logistic net, and unconventional tactics. However, with timely, accurate intelligence and persistent operations, interdiction can disrupt supply operations, destroy weapons caches and deny sanctuary. Additionally, most of the basic concepts for combat interdiction apply in noncombat environments. Whether the joint force is involved in major operations and campaigns or crisis response and limited contingency operations, interdiction actions such as direct attrition of enemy capabilities, constriction of enemy logistic systems, disruption of enemy C2 systems, forcing urgent movement upon the enemy, channeling enemy movements, denying enemy threat potential, and aiding in the enforcement of sanctions can create effects that achieve objectives. When developing interdiction objectives, consider the relationship between targets and what second or third order effects may be created, paying particular attention to potential unintended or undesired effects.

b. **Direct Attrition of Enemy Capabilities.** Interdiction against massed enemy forces can tip the operational advantage in favor of the friendly force. Attriting dispersed enemy forces and materiel may be difficult to execute because it requires locating individual targets. Modern weapons systems and sensors, however, can make this option more viable. In some cases, circumstances such as enemy deployment or limiting rules of engagement (ROE) may make fielded forces a more viable target than supporting infrastructure. Resources, terrain, weather, enemy actions, and characteristics are just a few variables to consider when developing interdiction targets.

(1) While a direct attack on individual enemy forces may be possible, it may not be the most efficient approach in terms of munitions and forces available. Although the direct destruction of individual enemy forces has an immediate impact on enemy combat power, it usually requires more assets due to the larger number of individual targets—especially if they are dispersed, concealed, or fortified. Isolating large enemy formations by destroying logistic nets, supplies, and supporting infrastructure can create the same effects with fewer resources.

(2) Terrain and weather affect the ability to attrite enemy forces. Attacking an enemy in open terrain in good weather significantly differs from striking an enemy in rough wooded terrain under a layer of foul weather. As an example, during Operation DESERT STORM, exposed Iraqi forces in open desert terrain were more vulnerable to interdiction by coalition airpower than dispersed Serbian forces that benefited from trees, valleys, and poor weather conditions during Operation ALLIED FORCE.

(3) Enemy characteristics influence the adopted concept of operations (CONOPS). The enemy's operational vulnerability and ability to replace losses—or adapt operations to mitigate them—must be weighed against the expected results of targeting supporting infrastructure. The enemy's movement also influences the ability to destroy fielded forces. Friendly maneuver can force an enemy to react and become predictable, making interdiction both viable and more effective.

c. **Constricting the Enemy Logistic System.** Combat creates demands on fielded forces and speeds consumption of vital war materiel. This in turn increases the effects of interdiction operations by straining the support systems and reducing stockpiles. For surface combat to take place, soldiers and their weapons, ammunition, food, and communications equipment must get to the battle. When the enemy consumes large quantities of supplies because of heavy combat or extensive movement, interdiction operations have an accelerated impact for two reasons. First, when opponents are under heavy pressure, they may be forced to use up stockpiles reserved for ongoing or future operations. Second, high consumption

---

INTERDICTION OPERATIONS IN THE BATTLE FOR AL KHAFJI

During the evening of 29 January 1991, the Iraqi Army sent elements of three divisions in motion southward out of their static positions in occupied Kuwait. While their ultimate objectives are not known, there is no question that all three advances were aimed at engaging coalition forces, with the largest ground battle developing in the Saudi town of Ra's Al Khafji.

While coalition forces engaged the Iraqi 5th Mechanized Division at Al Khafji, the two northern lines of the Iraqi advance suddenly found themselves very exposed, with their own movement serving to highlight themselves as targets. While Joint Surveillance Target Attack Radar System (JSTARS) located, tracked, and provided vectors to the columns of advancing Iraqi vehicles, coalition air interdiction missions took full advantage, using a variety of night vision devices and precision-guided munitions to inflict devastating damage and stop the Iraqi advance. After losing hundreds of vehicles and taking thousands of casualties, the Iraqis abandoned the attack as a costly failure. Intelligence, surveillance, and reconnaissance assets like the E-8 JSTARS (shown on the left) were vital in achieving the results depicted in the photograph to the right.

SOURCE: Stephen T. Hosmer, *Psychological Effects of US Air Operations in Four Wars, 1941-1991*

---

drives an enemy to use more direct routes, making it more vulnerable to interdiction attacks. The nature of ground combat also determines which supporting elements are most critical at any given time. Historically, an enemy army fighting under static conditions is more affected by the destruction of munitions, while a highly mobile enemy is more disrupted by the loss of fuel and transportation.

(1) The less surplus capacity the enemy's logistic systems have, the less they can compensate for damage. For any type of interdiction in a combat or noncombat

environment, degrading the mobility of the enemy's distribution system hinders its ability to redistribute assets to effectively counter friendly operations. When attacking the enemy's logistic systems, it is normally prudent to concentrate efforts on a small number of limiting factors such as concentrations of supplies; petroleum, oils, and lubricants; storage and resupply systems; or soft vehicles. **When a critical vulnerability is identified within the enemy's logistic systems, it is usually beneficial to employ parallel attacks against that vulnerability.**

(2) The enemy's transportation system must also be broken down into components when analyzing for weaknesses to attack. Most transportation systems consist of the actual conduit for travel (roads, rail, etc.), vehicles used to transport troops or supplies along the conduit, energy required for those vehicles to operate (typically petroleum or electricity), C2 to run the transportation system, and repair facilities to keep the system operating. The loading and unloading points in the transportation system may prove especially lucrative, as large concentrations of enemy forces or supplies are often found there. Examples include rail yards, harbors, and airfields. If forces or supplies are critically needed at the front, the enemy may not have the luxury of dispersing them during loading or unloading, which increases their vulnerability to interdiction. In many cases, the enemy will use the same transportation system for both forces and supplies. Under such circumstances, destroying or degrading the enemy's LOCs will affect both mobility and resupply capability. When analyzing an enemy transportation network for importance to its overall strategy, all possible uses for such a system must be considered. The analysis of the enemy's transportation network should include its surplus capacity and reconstitution capability.

d. **Disrupting Enemy C2.** The enemy's combat operations may be disrupted with strategic or interdiction attacks on their C2 nodes; the level of C2 disruption must be

A thorough assessment of the enemy's reconstitution capability is required.

commensurate with overall objectives. Attacks on the C2 structure may seek to isolate enemy combat forces from higher headquarters, or to force the enemy to use less capable and secure backup communications systems that can be more easily exploited. When the enemy employs a rigid, top-down C2 doctrine, it can be particularly vulnerable to the disruptive effects of C2 interdiction. This is especially true when the enemy has not had a long preparation period to exercise its plan, or when the conflict has moved beyond the initial stages. Conversely, an enemy that practices a high degree of C2 autonomy will likely be less affected by attacks on its C2 network. In some circumstances—such as a plan that includes forcing the enemy to react to friendly maneuver—complete destruction of the enemy C2 architecture could be counterproductive. The capability to affect the enemy through nonlethal information operations (IO) must also be considered, as this approach may lead to better overall results while freeing up conventional interdiction assets to prosecute alternate objectives.

e. **Forcing Urgent Movement Upon the Enemy.** The enemy may execute time urgent movement for several reasons: an attempt to achieve surprise, the need to attack before reinforcements or supplies arrive, the requirement for rapid reinforcement of threatened defensive positions, the attempt to exploit offensive operations, or when driven to urgent movement by interdiction. Rapid movement of enemy forces and supplies often makes them more vulnerable to interdiction. They generally become more concentrated while traversing more exposed and predictable avenues, foregoing time-consuming camouflage, concealment, and deception efforts. However, movements are normally limited in duration due to a desire to limit exposure. For friendly forces to capitalize on such opportunities, the JFC must deny the enemy mobility when it needs it most. Close coordination is required among all forces to take full advantage of the situation. Additionally, commanders require access to information systems able to process real-time and near real-time intelligence in order to exploit the capabilities of interdiction and the opportunities these operations create. Friendly forces must take full advantage of all reconnaissance and surveillance assets to detect when these movements occur.

f. **Channeling Enemy Movements.** Interdiction channels the enemy's movements. This is made easier by the lack of transportation routes, and man-made and natural obstacles. The fewer routes available to handle enemy supplies and reinforcements, the greater the loss or delay caused by severing those routes. Attacks on enemy lateral LOCs can channel movement, impair reinforcement, reduce operational cohesion, and create conditions for defeating the enemy in detail. Minefields may be employed to channel enemy maritime and ground movements, although our decision to use mines must be balanced against any potential that friendly forces or civilians may need to move through the targeted area. Geography may also restrict or channel surface movement, creating chokepoints and concentrated targets. Geography influences the rate of enemy movement, the size of the force to be moved, where it can move, and the means required to move the force. In cases where geography favors rapid movement of enemy forces, artificial and/or temporary chokepoints can be created by such means as delivery of large numbers of scatterable mines.

A detailed discussion of the integration of barriers, obstacles, and mines is included in Joint Publication (JP) 3-15, Barriers, Obstacles, and Mine Warfare for Joint Operations.

g. **Denying Enemy Threat Potential.** The presence or threat of effective interdiction operations can result in deterring a potential enemy's actions. Fear of interdiction can result in a less than optimum use of resources by the enemy. For example, an enemy that has faced or witnessed air interdiction (AI) may be reluctant to move reserve troops to the front lines where they are critically needed. The threat of interdiction operations is also a strong deterrent to the movement and proliferation of WMD. WMD interdiction encompasses operations directed toward weaponized chemical, biological, radiological, and nuclear devices/warheads and delivery vehicles; dual-use items required to produce devices/warheads, their precursors, or related items; related technology; financial and transportation intermediaries which facilitate trade in WMD; and individuals associated with all of the above. Actions to interdict/intercept WMD materiel occur throughout the operational area. The perceived effectiveness of friendly interdiction capabilities may provide a powerful deterrent to the proliferation of WMD or an enemy decision to employ WMD.

See Appendix B of JP 3-40, Combating Weapons of Mass Destruction, *for more information on WMD interdiction operations.*

h. **Enforcement of Sanctions.** Sanction enforcement operations employ coercive measures to interdict the movement of certain types of designated items or information into or out of a nation or specified area. Maritime interception operations (MIO) are a form of interdiction used for sanction enforcement that are military or legal in nature, and serve both political and military purposes. The political objective is to compel a country or group to conform to the objectives of the initiating body, while the military objective focuses on establishing a barrier that is selective, allowing only authorized goods or persons to enter or exit. Depending on the geography, sanction enforcement normally involves some combination of air and surface forces. MIO can be used across the range of military operations. It can be used to enforce sanctions or national policies imposed unilaterally, multinationally, or as directed by an intergovernmental organization (e.g., the United Nations Security Council) or other regional authority. MIO may include the following:

(1) Send armed boarding parties to visit merchant ships bound to, through, or out of a defined area.

(2) Examine merchant ships' documentation and cargo.

(3) Search for contraband.

(4) Divert vessels failing to comply with guidelines set by the sanctioning body.

(5) Seize vessels and cargo.

5. **Elements of Effective Interdiction**

Effective interdiction operations share a number of common elements that lead to the attainment of interdiction objectives. The mix of elements in each operation depends on such variables as the nature of the conflict, geographic location, weather, and enemy

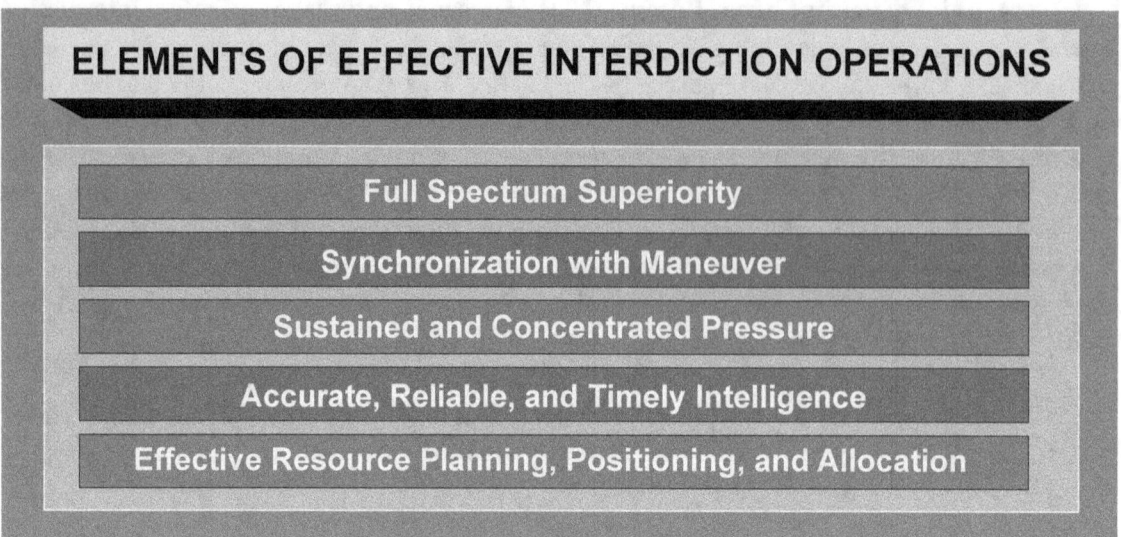

Figure I-1. Elements of Effective Interdiction Operations

characteristics. Elements normally required to successfully prosecute interdiction operations are shown in Figure I-1 and are discussed below.

a. **Full Spectrum Superiority.** The cumulative effect of dominance in the air, land, maritime, and space domains and information environment (which includes cyberspace) permits the conduct of joint operations without effective opposition or prohibitive interference.

b. **Synchronization with Maneuver.** An important factor for success is the synchronization of interdiction operations and maneuver. Planning and conducting interdiction and maneuver operations within a coherent framework creates a synergistic effect. The benefits of integrating these operations are discussed in more detail in Chapter III, "Joint Interdiction Planning."

c. **Sustained and Concentrated Pressure.** Successful interdiction operations have highlighted the importance of sustained, concentrated efforts. Since interdiction is often directed against replaceable systems or assets (vehicles, weapons, aircraft, ships, illegal/dangerous cargoes or persons, communications equipment) and reparable systems (engineering features, such as bridges and rail lines), sustained, concentrated pressure, sufficient to impede efforts to replace or repair affected assets, is required. This applies particularly to operations of long duration, because time allows the enemy to restore losses. Eventually, resourceful enemies can circumvent even the most enduring effects of interdiction. Success or failure often comes down to the balance between the enemy's ability to mitigate interdiction effects versus friendly ability to sustain interdiction actions. Attacks on key enemy repair and replacement assets may be advisable in many circumstances. Effective employment of intelligence, surveillance, and reconnaissance (ISR) assets provides critical information to the JFC on the results of interdiction and on the enemy's ability to reconstitute.

    d. **Accurate, Reliable, and Timely Intelligence.** Information about the enemy's plan of operations, LOCs, tactical dispositions, and capabilities is imperative to provide information about the enemy's probable course(s) of action (COA[s]), identify contraband shipments (as related to combating WMD) or interrelated target systems and allow the commander to anticipate enemy actions or counteractions and respond accordingly. A prerequisite for planning joint interdiction operations is an understanding of the capabilities and limitations of the enemy and how they are most likely to operate. Accurate, reliable, and timely intelligence allows commanders to develop achievable objectives, select appropriate targets, apply the appropriate weapon and delivery systems, and keep abreast of the enemy's response, as applicable.

    (1) Intelligence can provide interdiction operations with crucial input on target development by assessing enemy characteristics. Intelligence also supports interdiction planners with environmental assessments. Conversely, interdiction may enhance intelligence collection if, for example, the destruction of primary communications nets causes the enemy to use systems which are more vulnerable to exploitation.

    (2) Accurate, reliable, and timely intelligence is extremely important to maritime domain awareness (MDA). National Security Presidential Directive (NSPD)-41/Homeland Security Presidential Directive (HSPD)-13, *Maritime Security Policy*, defines MDA as "the effective understanding of anything associated with the global maritime domain that could impact the security, safety, economy, or environment of the United States." While an emerging capability, MDA is critical in enhancing our ability to identify threats in the maritime domain as early and as distant from our shores as possible by integrating intelligence, surveillance, observation, and navigation systems into a common operational picture throughout the United States Government (USG) and involved foreign nations. By networking maritime regions and resources into a common "global" maritime picture, useful data can be presented in a form that supports a wide range of planning, decision, execution, and assessment requirements to include those supporting interdiction operations. Given the nature of these operations, it is important that information be shared within the interagency and international communities to the maximum extent possible.

    e. **Effective Resource Planning, Positioning, and Allocation.** Ensuring the appropriate resources (units, munitions, vessels, etc.) are allocated and positioned to conduct effective interdiction operations requires detailed planning. Interdiction objectives will affect the movement and positioning of appropriate interdiction platforms and weapons. Proper weapon planning and employment are important factors for effective combat interdiction operations. Matching the correct weapon (system) to the target minimizes the time and resources required to achieve the objective. Mismatching available munitions or assets with targets and/or target systems can greatly increase the time and resources required to achieve the objectives of the interdiction operation, and unduly risks valuable personnel and weapon systems through additional strikes against the same undamaged/undestroyed target. Munitions and fuse settings should be tailored to the desired effect — target destruction, neutralization, or suppression. Although precision-guided munitions (PGMs) have become a primary weapon of choice, planners should realize that general purpose and cluster munitions may, consistent with application of ROE, create better effects in some situations. Planners should also consider the possibility of adverse weapons effects against friendly forces, such as the employment of time-delayed munitions against an enemy near advancing friendly forces. Additionally, planners should consider adverse effects of enemy munitions or weapons material collocated at a target site. Some WMD targets may have restrictions due to the danger of releasing contamination. PGMs are uniquely valuable in attacking hardened point targets or for minimizing collateral damage. These highly accurate munitions provide rapid strike capability with maximum flexibility, while standoff precision weapons allow joint interdiction forces to remain outside the most heavily defended areas with the same accuracies. Precision attack of key infrastructure, transportation, and C2 targets may cripple an enemy force's ability to maneuver. Furthermore, when the number of PGMs available is high enough, interdiction operations can inflict devastating losses on a mechanized enemy force. Such a strategy must consider the number of weapons required, the time required to achieve objectives, and whether more lucrative target sets exist.

CHAPTER II
JOINT INTERDICTION CAPABILITIES

> *"The line that connects an army with its base of supplies is the heel of Achilles—its most vital and vulnerable point."*
>
> **John S. Mosby, *War Reminiscences*, 1887**

1. Interdiction-Capable Forces

Interdiction operations can be conducted by all components of the joint force, across the range of military operations employing both lethal and nonlethal means. During interdiction operations, components may support or be supported by another component commander to achieve theater/JOA-wide interdiction objectives or they may conduct interdiction operations as part of their component mission. Forces that can conduct or be employed in interdiction operations include those listed in Figure II-1 and described below.

a. Air forces employ such weapons as projectiles, missiles, unguided munitions, PGMs, land and/or sea mines, electronic warfare (EW) systems, and sensors from airborne platforms in the AI role.

(1) AI is defined as air operations conducted to divert, disrupt, delay, or destroy the enemy's military surface capabilities before it can be brought to bear effectively against friendly forces, or to otherwise achieve objectives. AI is generally conducted at such distances from friendly forces that detailed integration of each AI mission with the fire and movement of friendly forces is not normally required. Some characteristics or considerations of AI follow.

(a) AI can be executed as a supported mission or it can provide support to surface commanders. AI contributes by disrupting the enemy's ability to command, mass, maneuver, withdraw, supply, and reinforce available combat power and by weakening the enemy physically and psychologically.

(b) AI can contribute to or achieve JFC objectives independent of surface forces. AI operations outside surface AO and conducted against enemy forces, LOCs, C2 systems, and other enemy resources can significantly alter the course of an operation.

(c) AI creates opportunities for friendly commanders to exploit. AI may support a surface scheme of maneuver within a surface commander's AO. By using JFC priorities, a surface component nominated target list, and a thorough understanding of the surface component's scheme of maneuver, AI can create effects that facilitate and support surface maneuver.

(d) AI is inherently less complicated to execute than close air support (CAS) because it does not require detailed integration with the fire and movement of friendly forces. Detailed integration requires extensive communications, comprehensive deconfliction procedures, and meticulous planning. Therefore, if the enemy surface force presents a

---

INTERDICTION-CAPABLE FORCES

Air forces employ such weapons as projectiles, missiles, unguided munitions, precision munitions, land and/or sea mines, electronic warfare systems, and sensors from airborne platforms.

Maritime forces employ assets such as surface combatants, carriers, amphibious shipping, aircraft, helicopters, submarines, landing forces, and special forces, and weapons such as missiles, munitions, torpedoes, and mines, capable of conducting a variety of air, land, and sea operations.

Land forces employ such assets as attack helicopters, missiles, artillery, and those forces capable of conducting conventional airborne, air assault, and amphibious operations.

Special operations forces may support conventional interdiction operations by providing terminal guidance for precision-guided munitions, or may act independently when the use of conventional forces is inappropriate or infeasible.

Other government agencies work with military forces in a "whole of government" approach to interdiction capabilities and forces. Military elements work with our interagency partners (Department of the Treasury, Federal Bureau of Investigation, etc.) to interdict threat finance and foreign fighter streams.

Figure II-1. Interdiction-Capable Forces

lucrative target, AI conducted before friendly land forces make contact can significantly degrade the enemy's fighting ability and reduce the number of CAS sorties required. The CAS/AI relationship has a parallel within the maritime domain. Like CAS, maritime air support (MAS) refers to air action against hostile surface targets—at sea—that requires detailed integration with the fire and movement of maritime forces. AI of maritime targets differs from MAS in that detailed tactical integration with naval surface forces is not required.

(2) Each Service's air forces' flexibility, range, speed, lethality, precision, and ability to mass at a desired time and place contribute significantly to the overall joint interdiction effort. Air forces offer the versatility and capability to deliver combat power against the enemy when and where needed to attain objectives across the range of military operations. The ability of aircraft to employ PGMs offers a distinct advantage over other weapon systems in many cases. PGMs can correct for ballistics, release, and targeting errors in flight. Explosive loads can also be more accurately tailored for the target, since planners can assume most bombs will strike in the manner and place expected. Unless using time-delayed munitions, manned and unmanned aircraft (UA) can offer the advantage of providing immediate attack assessment. Also, stealth aircraft and air-launched conventional

---

standoff weaponry reduce the risk of detection and loss of aircraft and aircrews while increasing the probability of successful attacks.

(3) Technological advancements have given the joint force UA armed with PGMs. UA have the benefit of lower cost, lower radar and visual signatures, and extended loiter times compared with most manned aircraft and provide the JFC another interdiction option, especially in heavily defended target areas. UA can be employed over suspected or known enemy strongholds to locate and engage targets of opportunity for longer periods of time. Armed UA have been used extensively in this capacity during Operation ENDURING FREEDOM (OEF) and Operation IRAQI FREEDOM (OIF).

(4) Employment of cluster munitions against land-based targets can increase the effectiveness of attacks. They allow a single aircraft to create desired effects on multiple pieces of equipment in a single pass. They also allow joint forces to channel the enemy into kill zones or deny access to an area. Sea mines can also be delivered by aircraft, deterring enemy ships from entering an area of the sea or sinking them. Often, mines are more effective for interdiction than bombs, because delayed effects munitions continue to be effective after the delivery aircraft have left the area. Enemy uncertainty regarding the presence of these munitions can result in excessive delays, diversion of resources into time-consuming countermeasures, and reduced enemy morale. However, the use of cluster/mine munitions may also present several disadvantages to the joint force to include: collateral damage, danger to civilians, post conflict cleanup cost, adverse coalition public relations implications, and denial of friendly access to the targeted area. Programmable self-destruct munitions may mitigate some of these disadvantages. The use of mines and cluster mines is

Air interdiction assets, such as this F-15E Strike Eagle, provide lethality, flexibility, and precision capabilities to the joint force.

governed by rigorous safeguards to ensure compliance with international law and the national security needs of the United States. US policy in this area is under constant review and modification. Employment must only be executed in accordance with the ROE approved for the operation. Additionally, the use of cluster/mine munitions may be problematic in an environment where multinational members have ratified international conventions against these munitions.

(5) Cruise missiles such as the conventional air-launched cruise missile (CALCM) can be effective interdiction assets and provide a potent employment option to the joint force. Several variants provide single warhead unitary blasts or a hardened target penetration warhead. Low risk, accuracy, and range make missiles most viable in the planning of interdiction contingency operations against stationary targets. CALCMs are capable of conducting short-notice strikes launched from aircraft operating outside the range of enemy threats. They are ideal for use against targets in heavily defended areas where the probability of the loss of manned aircraft is too high. CALCMs are also capable of neutralizing enemy air defenses to facilitate a much larger attack by land- and sea-based airpower.

(6) Joint forces employ EW in the form of electronic attack, electronic protection, and EW support to achieve the JFC's objectives, guidance, and intent. Examples of interdiction by EW systems include degrading, denying, and exploiting enemy C2 links with electromagnetic jammers, antiradiation missiles, and use of specialized sensors. EW systems may also intercept, maintain, and update enemy electronic order of battle data for use in subsequent operations. JP 3-13.1, *Electronic Warfare,* provides in-depth guidance for EW operations.

b. **Maritime forces employ missiles, torpedoes, fixed- and rotary-wing aircraft, mines, naval fires and boarding parties to support naval, air, and ground forces.** Ships performing surface warfare and submarines performing antisubmarine warfare are examples of interdiction actions to establish and maintain sea control. Interdiction in the maritime domain can isolate an enemy from outside support, halt undesired maritime activity, and enforce legal sanctions. It can also enhance free use of the sea LOCs for such friendly operations as deployment of forces and can provide security for other naval operations. Interdiction in the maritime domain can be significantly different from operations in other domains due to the complexity of international law of the sea. Especially when conducting homeland security (e.g., United States Coast Guard [USCG] under Title 14, United States Code [USC]) or homeland defense interdiction operations, maritime forces may be tasked to intercept, interdict, disable, stop, and board vessels prior to use of lethal means of interdiction.

(1) Missiles such as the Tomahawk land attack missile (TLAM) can be effective interdiction assets and provide a potent employment option to the joint force. TLAM is a long range, subsonic cruise missile used for land attack warfare, launched from surface ships and submarines. Low risk, accuracy, and range make missiles a viable option against stationary, non-hardened targets. TLAMs are capable of conducting short-notice strikes, without aircraft support, against targets in heavily defended areas where the probability of the loss of manned aircraft is too high. TLAMs are also capable of neutralizing enemy air defenses to facilitate a much larger attack by land- and sea-based airpower. In theater, the

maritime operations center—maritime headquarters Tomahawk strike and mission planning cells provide the joint force maritime component commander (JFMCC) with the capability to plan new missions or modify selected missions in the AO.

(2) Maritime interdiction can deny the enemy free movement into or within an objective area prior to an amphibious assault by landing force elements. Naval fires may also be used for interdiction along littoral LOCs.

(3) Interdiction of waterways can disrupt enemy infiltration, movement, and resupply along and across major waterways in an AO. Mines have a wide application to interdiction operations in both the littoral regions and the open ocean. They are effective in harbors, coastal regions, and strategic chokepoints of the ocean. Harbors can be vital to maintaining both a viable economy and an effective maritime force. A lack of adequate ports to resupply naval vessels may reduce the effectiveness of enemy forces. Ports may also be essential in sustaining a military campaign. Disrupting the flow of ships in and out of a port—or shutting it off altogether—can be an effective way to cripple an enemy.

(4) The general purpose of MIO is to interdict goods or persons prohibited by a lawful sanction. However, not every individual MIO action or boarding results in interdiction, because the vast majority of vessels boarded in these operations are free of prohibited goods or persons. While a primary mechanism for initiation of MIO has been United Nations Security Council resolutions, other rationales exist for MIO, including:

(a) consensual boarding (permission granted by the ship's captain);

(b) a flag state authorized boarding;

(c) an interception as a condition of port entry;

(d) the belligerent right of visit and search;

(e) an interception made in accordance with Article 110 of the Law of the Sea Convention to verify the vessel's flag and to determine if the voyage is in compliance with international law as it pertains to universal crimes (e.g., piracy, slave trade [quasi-universal crime] and unauthorized broadcasting); or

(f) an interception made pursuant to the right of self-defense.

(5) Bilateral ship boarding agreements—such as those negotiated between nations that have endorsed the Proliferation Security Initiative Statement of Interdiction Principles— can assist in the timely interdiction of vessels. The tactics, techniques, and procedures for the conduct of MIO are provided in Navy Tactics, Techniques, and Procedures (NTTP)/Coast Guard Publication 3-07.11, *Maritime Interception Operations,* which describes detailed visit, board, search, and seizure operations.

Tomahawk land attack missile launch from a Navy cruiser.

(6) Expanded maritime interception operations (EMIO) are authorized by the President and directed by the Secretary of Defense to deter, degrade, and/or disrupt or gather intelligence to prevent attacks against the US and its allies. EMIO involves interception of vessels identified to be transporting terrorists and/or terrorist-related materiel that pose an imminent threat to the United States and its allies. EMIO may be implemented without sanctions and may involve multinational forces or OGAs. The legal rationales required to permit boarding include those listed in subparagraph (4), above.

(7) Law enforcement operations (LEO) are a form of interdiction operations. The basis and mission of LEO, however, is different from MIO. Title 14, USC, gives the USCG statutory authority to make inquiries, examinations, inspections, searches, seizures, and arrests upon the high seas and waters over which the United States has jurisdiction for the prevention, detection, and suppression of violations of the laws of the United States. USCG vessels routinely conduct LEO independent of naval operations; however, Navy vessels may embark USCG law enforcement detachments (LEDETs) for boardings. Navy ships carrying LEDETs support federal law enforcement efforts, but Navy and other Department of Defense (DOD) personnel are generally prohibited from direct involvement in law enforcement activity, such as boarding, arrest, or seizure. Counterdrug and alien migrant interdiction operations are examples of LEO.

(8) Riverine operations facilitate interdiction in coastal and inland waterways. In areas with limited land transportation, but numerous waterways, rivers provide natural transportation routes and are logical population centers. In some developing countries, inland waterways are major arteries for economic circulation, and military operations may be

needed to keep waterways open to maintain the local economy. Water routes are strategically and tactically important to an insurgent or enemy force, particularly in situations where an external aggressor supports and directs insurgency. Such a situation dictates a doctrine and strategy of interdiction and control of waterways.

(a) A thorough understanding of the riverine environment is needed to plan and conduct riverine operations. In a riverine area, watercraft are the principal means of transport. In such areas, indigenous personnel often settle along the waterways because they are the only usable means of travel between villages. Civilian traffic and settlements conceal the enemy's movements and mining and ambush operations. Control of waterways is necessary in riverine areas.

(b) Riverine operations are joint operations undertaken primarily by ground and naval forces. Participating forces must coordinate and integrate efforts to achieve a common objective. Interdiction may be an objective of riverine operations, while other objectives may be to seize key terrain, strike, raid, or facilitate freedom of navigation. Mission, enemy, terrain and weather, troops, and support available—time available are the basis for the task organization. Considering the total forces available, riverine operations require a balance between types of forces. A special consideration in task organization for riverine operations is the amount of troop lift and fire support available from the air or maritime component or Army forces. The major factors determining maritime support requirements are:

1. The extent to which navigable waters permit moving naval support to, within, and around the AO.

2. The size of ground forces needed in the objective area, the availability of other means of transportation, and the desirability of using other means to deliver them.

3. The maritime commander having tactical control (TACON) of the movement and maneuver of watercraft under the operational control (OPCON) of the ground force commander being supported.

4. The maritime force commander having responsibility for moving subordinate joint force ships and watercraft between riverine bases and support facilities outside the riverine area. The land force commander in the riverine area is responsible for the security of ships within the area.

c. **Land forces employ such assets as attack helicopters, missiles, artillery, and forces capable of conducting conventional airborne, air assault, and amphibious operations.** Operational-level commanders isolate the AO by interdicting enemy military potential before its effective use against friendly forces. Firepower employed by land forces may be either direct or indirect. It is usually combined with maneuver for greatest effect and can be integrated with EW systems and other assets to divert, disrupt, delay, or destroy the enemy's military potential.

(1) Attack helicopters provide a commander with an effective and versatile means of interdicting enemy forces. They may use them for rapid reaction operations and where

*AH-64 Apache attack helicopters are an organic Army asset
that can be used for interdiction missions.*

terrain restricts or prohibits ground force occupation or engagement of the enemy's forces. Attack helicopters are capable of employing precision-guided weapons and providing terminal guidance for other interdiction forces. They are capable of operating during the day or night and in adverse weather conditions.

(2) Missile systems such as Army Tactical Missile System (ATACMS) are very effective assets for interdicting high value, well-defended targets, day or night, in all weather conditions. ATACMS provides the joint force with a flexible employment option which can complement and enhance the theater/JOA-wide interdiction effort. They can conduct short-notice strikes without airborne aircraft support against targets in heavily defended areas where the probability of the loss of manned aircraft is too high. Missile systems are usually employed against soft, stationary targets. These targets include unhardened surface-to-surface missile sites, emplaced artillery batteries, air defense sites, logistic sites, and C2 facilities. Current technology for missile system warhead guidance allows missiles to target mobile armor formations and small point targets such as buildings or other non-hardened targets.

(3) Although artillery primarily provides close supporting fires to the maneuver force, it can also provide a significant contribution to interdiction operations. Artillery can create obstacles to enemy maneuver and cover the friendly force's advance with smoke and

fire. Artillery can suppress enemy defensive systems to facilitate ground and air operations, and can be used to promote deception, keep the enemy off balance, interdict enemy counterattack routes, and test its responses. Appropriate artillery target areas include mobility corridors which form chokepoints on the enemy supply route and areas through which hostile weapon systems and equipment must pass. Artillery systems such as the multiple launch rocket system (MLRS) can be extremely effective against a variety of targets, and are capable of keeping up with fast-paced maneuver advances. Guided MLRS rockets and 155-millimeter Excalibur projectiles provide a commander a coordinate seeking weapon to use when precision is required for a specific target.

(4) Airborne and air assault forces provide the joint force with an interdiction capability, using forcible entry operations in the form of raids to seize key terrain or chokepoints to achieve interdiction objectives. During Operation DESERT STORM, elements of the XVIII Airborne Corps, in the largest air assault in military history, penetrated 260 kilometers into Iraqi territory to the Euphrates River. The purpose of this operation was to cut the Iraqi LOCs along Highway 8 to Baghdad, effectively isolating Iraqi forces in the Kuwait theater of operations.

d. **Special Operations Forces.** SOF are employed as an interdiction force when the use of conventional forces is inappropriate or infeasible. SOF may also be used in conjunction with conventional forces to enhance interdiction operations. SOF are generally unconventional in nature and often clandestine in character, which makes them uniquely qualified to conduct interdiction against irregular threats. SOF may conduct coastal or riverine interdiction operations using a variety of special operations ships and craft. In a

This night multiple launch rocket system attack shows the overwhelming firepower that can be directed at interdiction targets.

linear operational environment, SOF may be inserted in the enemy's rear operations area for their disruptive effect or to take out key transitory targets. Such direct action operations typically involve an attack on critical targets such as LOCs. SOF may employ organic weapon systems such as fixed- or rotary-winged gunships. Additionally, SOF may enlist the support of local friendly forces who may interdict from within the enemy's infrastructure in areas presumed to be safe from attack. SOF may also degrade or obstruct the warmaking capability of a country by damaging, destroying, or diverting war materiel, facilities, utilities, and resources. This sabotage may be the most effective or only means of attacking specific targets that lie beyond the capabilities of conventional weapon systems. SOF are a potent interdiction force in their own right, as discussed earlier. However, their greatest contribution to joint interdiction operations may be in their use as a force enabler and multiplier. **SOF complement and support conventional interdiction operations by providing intelligence, target cueing, guidance for PGMs, and post attack assessment.**

(1) The use of SOF in terminal guidance operations (TGO) can significantly enhance interdiction. TGO are actions that provide additional information regarding a specific target location to approaching aircraft and/or weapons by electronic, mechanical, voice, or visual communications. This combination of SOF TGO and joint interdiction aircraft was used extensively during OEF.

(2) SOF special reconnaissance (SR) missions are another means of supporting interdiction operations. SR is reconnaissance and surveillance actions conducted as a special operation in hostile, denied, or politically sensitive environments to collect or verify information of strategic or operational significance, employing military capabilities not normally found in conventional forces. These actions provide an additive capability for commanders and supplement other conventional reconnaissance and surveillance actions. Even with today's sophisticated long-range sensors and overhead platforms, some information can be obtained only by visual observation or other collection methods in the target area. SOF's highly developed capabilities of gaining access to denied and hostile areas, worldwide communications, and specialized aircraft and sensors enable SR against targets inaccessible to other forces or assets. SR is further divided into two mission subsets:

(a) **Target Acquisition (TA).** TA includes all activities to acquire and collect information in support of planning for or interdiction of a specific target. These actions can be in support of a follow on SOF mission or in support of other strike assets.

<u>1</u>. **Reconnaissance.** These are operations with the primary purpose of locating targets of opportunity, e.g., enemy materiel, personnel, and facilities in assigned general areas or along assigned ground communication routes, and LOCs. Reconnaissance is not conducted for the purpose of attacking specific identified targets.

<u>2</u>. **Target and Threat Assessment.** These are operations conducted to detect, identify, locate, and assess a target to determine the most effective employment of weapons. This type of operation might include the assessment of the potential effects (to include collateral damage) of a strike or an attack on a chemical, biological, radiological, nuclear, or toxic industrial material site.

AC-130 Gunship

(b) **Specific Data Collection.** Specific data collection consists of all activities to collect data for purposes other than targeting.

<u>1</u>. **Environmental Reconnaissance.** These are operations conducted to collect and report critical hydrographic, geological, and meteorological information.

<u>2</u>. **Post Strike Reconnaissance.** SOF can gather a variety of post-interdiction information, including general atmospherics, impact on population behavior, and detailed battle damage assessment (BDA) on target structures.

e. **Other Government Agencies.** Often, DOD will either support or be supported by OGAs. Supporting combatant commands or government agencies can provide capabilities in support of interdiction. When these capabilities are synchronized with global ISR and IO, they play a key role in the interdiction of WMD and other forms of interdiction. USG departments such as the Department of State, Department of Energy, Department of Homeland Security (DHS), and Department of the Treasury bring significant resources to the table in the effort for interdiction. The JFC should coordinate through the combatant commander to access these resources.

See JP 3-08, Interorganizational Coordination During Joint Operations, *for further information.*

2. Complementary Operations

Joint interdiction operations are most effective when fully integrated with other air, land, sea, space, information, and special operations of the joint force. In addition to counterair and maneuver, other operations notable for their specialized roles which can complement joint interdiction operations include the following:

a. **Strategic Attack Operations.** A strategic attack is a JFC-directed offensive action against a target—whether military, political, economic, or other—that is specifically selected to achieve national or military strategic objectives. These attacks seek to weaken the enemy's ability or will to engage in conflict or continue an action and as such, could be part of a campaign, major operation, or conducted independently as directed by the President. Additionally, these attacks may achieve strategic objectives without necessarily having to achieve operational objectives as a precondition. Suitable targets may include but are not limited to enemy strategic centers of gravity (COGs). Strategic attack and interdiction operations complement one another. As an example, strategic attack may focus on halting production and storage of critical war materiel, while interdiction concentrates on cutting off the flow of this materiel. Strategic attack and interdiction operations also create a synergistic effect with simultaneous attacks against the enemy in depth, which places maximum stress on the enemy, allowing them no respite.

b. **Intelligence, surveillance, and reconnaissance** is an activity that synchronizes and integrates the planning and operation of sensors, assets, and processing, exploitation, and dissemination systems in direct support of current and future operations. This is an integrated intelligence and operations function, and comprises a joint mission to produce relevant information from all sources in a comprehensive, responsive, timely manner, so that military decision makers may gain and maintain an information advantage over an enemy.

c. **Space Operations.** Space operations facilitate and enhance interdiction operations. Space systems support joint interdiction target analysts, planners, and combat forces by providing capabilities for C2; sea, land, and space surveillance; intelligence collection; tactical warning and combat assessment; navigation; geospatial information and services; and environmental monitoring. Denying the enemy access to its space capabilities and attacking the enemy's capabilities to deny US and partner nation space capabilities must be integrated into joint interdiction plans and operations. Planning must take into account possible reliability and vulnerability issues of space-based systems. Joint force reliance on these systems makes them a lucrative target for an enemy with the means to attack them. Also, many space-based systems, such as global positioning system signals, are susceptible to EW techniques and environmental interference, and these factors must be taken into account during the planning process.

JP 3-14, Space Operations, *provides further amplification on the role of space forces in joint operations.*

d. **Information Operations.** IO are the integrated employment of the core capabilities of EW, computer network operations, military information support operations (MISO), military deception, and operations security, in concert with specified supporting and related capabilities, to influence, disrupt, corrupt, or usurp adversarial human and automated decision making while protecting our own. **IO complements interdiction through a variety of means and can be used to accomplish interdiction objectives, ideally achieving the goals before friendly forces engage the enemy.** The growing dependence on

Air refueling is a key part of most air interdiction operations and extends the range, payload, and endurance of air interdiction assets, thereby increasing their effectiveness.

information, information technology systems, and cyberspace by all forces and functions creates opportunities to use IO against the enemy. Use of IO to attack C2, logistic, or intelligence functions may lead to confusion, uncertainty, or lack of confidence in information systems and may contribute directly to collapse of enemy capability and will. Disrupting the enemy's communications and other systems within the operational environment cripples the enemy's ability to direct organized operations or leverage information systems to its advantage. Additionally, the synergistic effects of MISO conducted in parallel with interdiction operations can attack the enemy's will to fight simultaneously. The psychological shock of massed joint interdiction and IO can be overwhelming to the enemy's fielded forces, especially when those forces have already been strained by surface combat. **The nonlethal nature of many IO capabilities allows their use prior to and after hostilities, extending contact across time, thereby giving the friendly force greater opportunity to influence events and outcomes favorably.**

Chairman of the Joint Chiefs of Staff Instruction (CJCSI) 3210.01, Joint Information Operations Policy, *and JP 3-13*, Information Operations, *discuss the role of IO in joint warfare.*

e. **Air refueling** provides the JFC the ability to maneuver and mass interdiction forces, using surprise and economy of force, at a time and location where the enemy is least prepared, to deter, dissuade, or destroy. Station times will be increased for airborne, on call AI missions, providing decreased response times. While technically a "support" asset, air refueling has become such an integrated part of interdiction force packaging that it would be difficult to imagine operating without the enhanced capabilities it provides. For example, enemy antiship defenses may force an aircraft carrier to stand off from the target area,

E-3 airborne warning and control aircraft are invaluable in the sequencing of air interdiction assets to strike coordination and reconnaissance missions.

requiring refueling support to get carrier aviation to the fight. When air superiority is in dispute and enemy aircraft and missiles threaten air bases close to the fight, air refueling may be the only way to get interdiction missions to the target area.

f. **Strike Coordination and Reconnaissance (SCAR).** SCAR is a mission flown for the purpose of detecting targets and coordinating or performing attack or reconnaissance on those targets. SCAR missions are flown in a specific geographic area and are an element of the C2 interface to coordinate multiple AI flights, detect and attack targets, neutralize enemy air defenses, and provide BDA. The area may be defined by a box or grid where potential targets are known or suspected to exist, or where mobile enemy surface units have relocated because of surface fighting. SCAR coordinators perform a similar function for AI missions that forward air controller (airborne) (FAC[A]) provides for CAS aircraft. **Typical SCAR tasks include cycling multiple attacking flights through the target area and providing prioritized targeting guidance and enemy air defense updates to maximize the effect of each sortie.** SCAR in the maritime environment is directed by a SCAR coordinator (airborne or surface based) as specified by the surface warfare commander (SUWC). Although fighter aircraft often accomplish SCAR missions, the Joint Surveillance Target Attack Radar System (JSTARS) can perform SCAR tasks such as locating, verifying, and

> *"Both Afghanistan and Iraq were air mobility wars. Every single flight into these areas of operation needed some kind of air refueling—fighters, bombers, lifters, and even other tankers needed air refueling."*
>
> **General John W. Handy,**
> **Commander, United States Transportation Command,**
> **October 2001–September 2005**

cross-cueing other assets to positively identify moving targets; procedurally controlling and sequencing aircraft; and passing target updates. Additionally, the control and sequencing of aircraft are best performed by an E-3 airborne warning and control system, an E-2C carrier based C2 aircraft, or a ground-based control and reporting center. Even though some SCAR responsibilities are similar to that of a FAC/FAC(A), unless specifically qualified, SCAR coordinators do not have the authority to control CAS. Detailed SCAR procedures are outlined in Field Manual (FM) 3-60.2, Marine Corps Reference Publication (MCRP) 3-23C, NTTP 3-03.4.3, Air Force Tactics, Techniques, and Procedures (Instruction) (AFTTP[I]) 3-2.72, *Multi-Service Tactics, Techniques, and Procedures for Strike Coordination and Reconnaissance.*

Intentionally Blank

CHAPTER III
JOINT INTERDICTION PLANNING

"A good plan violently executed now is better than a perfect plan next week."

George S. Patton, Jr., *War As I Knew It*, 1947

1. Overview

The JFC directs the actions of air, land, maritime, space, and SOF to achieve objectives through an integrated joint campaign and major operations. The manner in which the JFC plans, organizes, and directs forces affects the responsiveness and versatility of joint interdiction operations. Unity of effort, centralized planning, and decentralized execution are key to success in joint and interagency interdiction operations.

a. **Joint Force Objectives.** JFCs employ forces to accomplish their objectives; the principal challenge is to combine force capabilities and operations to create effects that support achievement of those objectives. The planning, coordination, and integration of joint interdiction with other operations, such as maneuver, can yield unique advantages. This integration of effort begins with the JFC's theater/JOA-level objectives, guidance, and intent. Likewise, the JFC's theater/JOA campaign or operation plan facilitates such integration and helps to ensure that interdiction operations are part of a larger design aimed at achieving the JFC's objectives. Centralized planning and decentralized execution of joint interdiction operations ensure coherence and aid in the effective use of force; enhance the exploitation of tactical events; avoid fragmented, duplicated, and conflicting efforts; and accommodate the Service and functional components' different employment concepts and procedures.

b. Joint interdiction typically focuses on operational level objectives as delineated in the JFC's operation or campaign plans. It must also support strategic level objectives by working in concert with other efforts to neutralize or destroy the enemy's COGs or other key target systems. Additionally, joint interdiction complements maneuver force operations. Successful joint interdiction requires close integration with other operations, available resources, and anticipated effects. Strategic and operational level objectives are best described in terms of desired outcomes rather than specific targets.

c. Simultaneity in planning refers to the simultaneous application of military and nonmilitary power against the enemy's critical capabilities/requirements and COGs. Simultaneity in joint force operations contributes directly to an enemy's collapse by placing more demands on enemy forces and functions than can be handled. To the degree possible within the constraints of the principles of economy of force and mass, joint force operations should be conducted across the full breadth and depth of the operational area, creating competing and simultaneous demands on enemy commanders and resources. Just as with simultaneity, the concept of depth seeks to overwhelm the enemy throughout the operational area; creating competing and simultaneous demands on enemy commanders and resources and contributing to the enemy's speedy defeat. Interdiction is one manner in which JFCs add depth to operations at the operational level. This also forms the foundation of deep operations theory. The intent of deep operations is to bring force to bear on the opponent's entire structure, at the tactical, operational, and strategic depths, in a near simultaneous manner. The goal is to compel the enemy to comply with our will by diminishing its freedom to act and to resist our intentions through a continual erosion of its own capabilities and will. Operational reach enables early detection and identification of threats and increases the opportunity for interdiction.

d. Geographic distance (that is, "close" versus "deep") should not constitute the primary distinction between different forms of interdiction. The concept of depth applies to time as well as space. Operations extended in depth, in time as well as space, shape future conditions and can disrupt an opponent's decision cycle. Although it has usually been the case that interdiction closer to surface forces was designed to affect the battle over a shorter term than actions deeper in the enemy's territory, the most important aspect in planning interdiction operations is the effect desired, which may be measured in time. Once objectives, guidance, intent, and desired effects are known, commanders can make appropriate targeting decisions.

e. **Immediacy of Interdiction Operations.** The relative immediacy of the impact of interdiction may depend on several factors: the distance between interdiction operations and the location of intended effect, the means and rate of enemy movement (ships, trains, aircraft, trucks, tanks, or foot), the type of interdiction targets (forces, supplies, fuel, munition, or infrastructure), the level of enemy activity, and the strength and resilience of the attacked force or system. The JFC should not apply strict geographic boundaries to interdiction, but should plan for its theater/JOA-wide application.

2. Command Relationships

JFCs typically conduct joint interdiction operations through component commanders. All elements of the joint force can be called upon to perform interdiction operations. For example, SOF may conduct limited interdiction operations deep in enemy territory, and land or maritime force commanders may employ interdiction assets within their AOs. Planning and coordinating interdiction operations occurs at many levels of command within a joint force. The flexibility and capability of interdiction-capable assets allow them to be employed in a multitude of situations. Subordinate commanders possess organic assets which can contribute to interdiction operations. These assets may also be employed in support of the JFC's operation or campaign objectives, or to support other components of the joint force, which benefits the joint force as a whole. Normally, air assets tasked in support of the theater/JOA-wide interdiction effort are also heavily tasked to conduct or support other joint operations, such as CAS, counterair, strategic attack, IO, and maritime support.

a. **Unity of Effort in Joint Interdiction Operations.** The capabilities of forces used for joint interdiction, as well as the magnitude of their potential contribution, must be considered while planning and conducting the joint interdiction effort. The JFC structures the joint force to ensure that diverse component capabilities, operations, and forces complement each other to achieve the desired results effectively and efficiently. **To ensure unity of command and effort of air operations throughout a theater/JOA, the JFC normally delegates the planning and execution of theater/JOA-wide AI operations to** the component commander, with the preponderance of AI assets with theater/JOA-wide range and the ability to control them. The joint force air component commander (JFACC) is normally the supported commander for the JFC's overall AI effort, while land and maritime component commanders are supported commanders for interdiction in their AOs.

b. **The JFC establishes JFACC authority and command relationships.** JFACC authorities and command relationships typically include exercising OPCON over assigned and attached forces (through the Service component commander) and TACON over other military capabilities and/or forces made available for tasking. However, the JFC may decide that direct support is a more appropriate command authority for certain capabilities and/or forces.

c. **JFC Staff Option.** There may be situations in which designation of a JFACC is not required when a conflict or situation is of limited duration, scope, or complexity. If this option is exercised by the JFC, the JFC's staff will assist in planning and coordinating interdiction operations for JFC approval.

Refer to JP 3-30, Command and Control for Joint Air Operations, *for a detailed discussion of command relationships involving joint air operations. For more information on command relationships and authorities, see JP 1,* Doctrine for the Armed Forces of the United States.

d. **The Maritime Operational Threat Response (MOTR) plan for the National Strategy for Maritime Security provides guidance for an integrated network of national-level maritime command centers** to achieve coordinated, unified, timely, and effective planning and mission accomplishment by the USG. This integrated network consists of existing command or operations centers of the MOTR agencies, at the national level, to ensure a coordinated response consistent with desired national outcomes. MOTR addresses the full range of maritime security threats, including actionable knowledge of acts of terrorism, piracy, and other criminal or hostile acts committed by state and nonstate actors. In the maritime arena, the MOTR plan:

(1) Directs the establishment of an integrated network of national-level maritime command centers to achieve coordinated, unified, timely, and effective planning and mission accomplishment.

(2) Sets forth lead and supporting federal agency roles and responsibilities for MOTR based on existing law, desired USG outcome, greatest potential magnitude of the threat, the response capabilities required, asset availability, and authority to act. Some of the applicable interdiction roles and responsibilities of the MOTR plan include:

(a) DOD is the pre-designated lead MOTR agency for tactical response and resolution of nation-state threats within the maritime domain.

(b) DOD is the pre-designated lead MOTR agency for maritime terrorist threats that occur in the forward maritime areas of responsibility. DOD will be prepared to take a lead or supporting role for response to maritime terrorist threats globally as part of the USG's active, layered defense of the US.

(c) DHS is the pre-designated lead MOTR agency for the interdiction of maritime threats in waters where DHS normally operates, except as otherwise noted in the plan.

(d) These pre-designated leads can shift to another MOTR agency dependent on changes in desired outcome or availability of assets.

(3) Directs clear coordination relationships and operational coordination requirements among the lead and supporting MOTR agencies. The MOTR coordination process is conducted through a virtual network of interagency national and operational command centers. This process includes protocols for interagency coordination, consultation, and assessment throughout MOTR execution. The MOTR protocols and procedures allow rapid response to short-notice (pop-up) threats and require interagency partners to begin coordination activities (i.e., MOTR conference calls) at the earliest possible opportunity when one of the following triggers is met:

(a) Any terrorist or foreign state threat exists and US agency response is anticipated.

(b) More than one federal department or agency has become or must become substantially involved in responding to the threat.

(c) A single agency or department either lacks capability, capacity, or jurisdiction to address the threat.

(d) Upon resolving the threat, the initial responding federal department or agency cannot execute the disposition of cargo, people, or vessels acting under their own authority.

(e) The threat poses a potential adverse effect on the foreign affairs of the United States.

(4) This coordination process determines which agency is the right choice for leading the USG's response and what other agencies are needed to support the response effort. Additionally, this process includes protocols for transition of the lead from one agency to another and dispute resolution (i.e., if the USG's desired outcome cannot be resolved at the lower levels of government [e.g., operational level], the characterization of a particular threat could ultimately be elevated for Presidential resolution). At the tactical level, it is important to realize that the MOTR process exists not only to achieve the USG's desired outcome, but to coordinate and assist in bringing additional capabilities to bear on a threat.

e. **USCG.** Although a part of DHS, USCG is a military Service and a branch of the Armed Forces of the United States (Title 14, USC, Section 1 and Title 10, USC, Section 101). The USCG is at all times an "armed force" under Title 14, USC. The USCG does not require Title 10, USC, authority to participate in the national defense of the United States. Upon declaration of war, or when directed by the President, the USCG transfers to the Department of the Navy (Title 14, USC, Section 2). Even after transfer, the USCG retains full Title 14, USC, authorities. Absent such declaration or direction, the Service operates under the auspices of DHS and closely cooperates with the Navy regarding maritime security issues (Title 14, USC, Section 145) and assists DOD in the performance of any activity for which the USCG is especially qualified.

f. **Component commanders develop interdiction priorities to enhance mission accomplishment.** The land and maritime force commanders are the supported commanders within the AOs designated by the JFC. Within their designated AOs, land and maritime component commanders integrate and synchronize joint maneuver and fires functions, and interdiction missions. To facilitate this integration and synchronization, such commanders have the authority to designate target priority, effects, and timing of fires within their AOs. Within their AOs, commanders attempt to strike interdiction targets with organic assets first when practical and feasible. Coordination with the JFACC in these instances may be necessary to prevent redundant targeting and joint interdiction mission disruption. Interdiction targets which the land or maritime force commander is unable to strike, due to lack of organic assets or for which joint force interdiction assets are best suited, are nominated to the joint targeting process as individual targets, categories of targets, or in terms of desired effects. Once validated, the targets may be prosecuted by another component commander or another component commander's assets may be made available for tasking to the air, land, or maritime force commander. However, forwarding desired effects rather than strict target nominations gives those responsible for conducting joint interdiction maximum flexibility to exploit their capabilities.

(1) **The supported commander should clearly articulate the concept of maneuver operations to commanders who apply joint interdiction forces within the commander's designated AO.** In particular, supported commanders should provide supporting commanders as much latitude as possible in planning and executing their operations. When coordinating maneuver operations, supported commanders should clearly state how they envision interdiction supporting their maneuver operations, what they want to accomplish with interdiction, as well as those actions they want to avoid, such as the destruction of key transportation nodes or the use of certain munitions in a specific area.

(2) Supported commanders can determine specific targets for interdiction conducted within their AOs or, most preferably, give supporting commanders mission-type instructions in order to provide the other components as much leeway as possible. For example, the joint force land component commander (JFLCC) could indicate to the JFACC that an advancing enemy tank division is automatically the highest priority. The JFACC can then determine how best to support the JFLCC—without knowing in advance the exact location or timing of the priority target. **By judiciously employing fire support coordination measures (FSCMs), commanders can facilitate the joint interdiction effort within their assigned AOs.**

(3) **It is important to note that joint interdiction can be conducted inside an AO in direct response to JFC tasking, and may not be in support of the AO commander.** The JFC may, for example, have designated certain high-payoff targets that are located inside a subordinate commander's AO. Any commander executing such a mission within a land or maritime AO must coordinate the operation to avoid adverse effects

---

GULF WAR COALITION INTERDICTION

Coalition air interdiction operations placed Iraqi forces on the horns of a dilemma: if they remained in position, they would be struck either from the air or by the advancing Coalition ground forces; if they tried to move, they made themselves extremely vulnerable to patrolling Coalition aircraft, including attack helicopters.

SOURCE: Department of Defense Final Report to Congress
on the Conduct of the Persian Gulf War

---

and fratricide. If those operations would have an adverse impact within a land or maritime AO, the commander assigned to execute the mission must readjust the plan, resolve the issue with the land or maritime component commander, or consult with the JFC for resolution.

3. **Integrating Interdiction and Maneuver**

a. Interdiction and maneuver operations are potent entities in their own right. Both maneuver and interdiction operations include the movement of forces and weapon systems, and delivery of fires (lethal and nonlethal) which create effects to support objectives at all levels through the range of military operations. Maneuver and interdiction could be conducted relatively independent of each other in certain circumstances. **However, integrating interdiction and maneuver, as well as their joint fires, enhances the ability for each to more fully contribute to a successful outcome of a campaign or major operation.**

b. **Interdiction and maneuver are complementary operations that should normally be integrated to create dilemmas for the enemy.** Synchronizing AI with a ground movement toward the enemy flank forces the enemy into the dilemma of either absorbing a potentially deadly flanking ground attack or repositioning and exposing themselves to a much more effective air attack. Accordingly, integrating interdiction and maneuver provides one of the most dynamic concepts available to the joint force. **Interdiction and maneuver should not be considered as separate operations against a common enemy, but rather as complementary operations designed to achieve the JFC's objectives.**

(1) Maneuver can play a major role in enabling conditions for effective employment of interdiction. Maneuver can place sustained pressure on the enemy, forcing the enemy to increase consumption of logistics, increasing resupply rates and thereby increasing frequency of exposure to interdiction. As a result, interdiction may destroy enemy forces and assets at a faster rate than they can be repaired, replaced, or resupplied. Actual or threatened maneuver can force an enemy to respond by attempting rapid repositioning or resupply. **Close coordination among the components will help ensure that conditions occur in which the enemy force is made most vulnerable to interdiction.**

(2) **Joint interdiction can also facilitate maneuver operations.** It may, but does not have to, occur at the same place and time as the maneuver to be effective. Joint interdiction can control the time of engagement to that point most advantageous to friendly

---

forces. Joint interdiction can be a major contributor and enabler for land and naval force operations. Interdiction can give surface forces the time and protection they need to maneuver. The psychological effects of interdiction efforts can greatly reduce the will of enemy forces to continue, especially when faced with the prospect of having to defend against subsequent maneuver operations. In a forced entry scenario, joint interdiction may support land and amphibious maneuver operations by denying the enemy supply or resupply of equipment and forces to the objective area. It may also interfere with their means of C2 or provide a diversionary screen. Joint interdiction can isolate enemy forces, control the movement of enemy forces into or out of a land or maritime AO, and set conditions for maneuver forces. When joint interdiction is conducted in support of land or maritime forces, it should be properly integrated with the scheme of maneuver of the supported force. Within the AO, the supported land or maritime commander is responsible for the integration of maneuver, fires, and interdiction. To facilitate this synchronization, such commanders designate the target priority, effects, and timing of interdiction operations within their AOs.

c. **The JFC ultimately approves the integration of joint interdiction operations with the execution of other joint force operations.** JFACC controlled interdiction operations conducted over maritime and littoral areas may require close coordination between the JFACC and the JFMCC. Additionally, in the case of AI operations short of the fire support coordination line (FSCL), all air-to-ground and surface-to-surface attack operations are controlled by the appropriate land or amphibious force commander. Coordination between the JFACC and the JFLCC, as well as coordination between aircrews and friendly surface forces, is required through the appropriate air C2 agencies.

4. **Planning Joint Interdiction**

a. The JFC establishes broad planning objectives and guidance for interdiction of enemy forces as an integral part of a joint campaign or major operation. Subordinate commanders recommend to the JFC how to use their combat power more effectively to this end. With this advice, the JFC sets interdiction priorities, provides targeting guidance, and makes apportionment decisions. The JFC should clearly designate where the weight of the joint interdiction should be applied. Weight of effort may be expressed in terms of percentage of total available resources; by assigning priorities for resources used with respect to other aspects of the theater/JOA campaign or operation; or as otherwise determined by the JFC. This is a particularly important consideration for commanders who must determine the correct number and types of forces and weapon systems within their AO, including the effects of joint interdiction. Likewise, effective interdiction planners must have a thorough understanding of the JFC's CONOPS. Once the JFC establishes campaign or major operation objectives, component commanders develop operation plans that accomplish (or contribute to the accomplishment of) the theater/JOA-wide strategic and operational objectives. Commanders should consider how planned operations can complement joint interdiction objectives and vice versa. These operations may include such actions as deception operations, withdrawals, lateral repositioning, and flanking movements that are likely to cause the enemy to maneuver large surface forces which may make them more vulnerable to interdiction.

b. **Component Organic Interdiction Operations.** Components may conduct interdiction operations as part of their specific mission in addition to, or in lieu of, supporting the theater/JOA-wide interdiction effort. For example, maritime forces charged with seizing and securing a lodgment along a coast may include the interdiction of opposing land and maritime forces as part of the overall amphibious operation. Within an assigned AO, a ground commander can interdict enemy forces to enhance the effects of the friendly scheme of maneuver with the use of such organic assets as ATACMS, organic fixed- and rotary-wing aircraft, and artillery. In such situations as these, C2 for the operation is normally conducted according to the component's procedures.

c. **Joint Force Air Component Commander.** The JFACC recommends theater/JOA-wide air targeting priorities as assigned and, in coordination with other component commanders' interdiction priorities, forwards the air apportionment recommendation to the JFC. The JFC provides target priorities and air apportionment guidance to the JFACC and other component commanders. **The JFACC, using priorities established in the JFC's air apportionment decision, then plans and executes the overall AI effort, using air assets assigned or made available.**

(1) Theater/JOA AI capabilities and forces made available for tasking are determined by the JFC, in consultation with component commanders. They are based on JFC-assigned objectives and the CONOPS. Following the JFC's air apportionment decision, the JFACC allocates and tasks the capabilities/forces made available. **The JFACC's AI employment guidance, based on the JFC's air apportionment decision, is used by the joint air operations center (JAOC) for input into the air tasking order (ATO).** Aircraft or other capabilities and forces not allocated for tasking should be included in the ATO for coordination purposes. These may be redirected only with the approval of the JFC or affected component commander. The ATO process assists the JFACC in synchronizing, planning, and executing the overall air effort. The air apportionment process and the air tasking cycle are discussed further in JP 3-30, *Command and Control for Joint Air Operations.*

(2) The JFC is the only individual who has the authority to change the air apportionment decision. However, the JFACC may divert, cancel, or change apportioned AI target assignments to adapt to a changing situation, consistent with the JFC's intent. Although such changes are not considered "changing the air apportionment," the JFACC coordinates changes with affected commanders whenever possible to minimize impact on other joint force operations. The JFC may give the JFACC the authority to redirect joint air operations, but **the JFC or affected component commander must approve all requests for redirection of direct support air assets.** Affected component commanders will be notified by the JFACC upon redirection of joint sorties previously allocated in the joint ATO for support of component operations.

d. In the maritime domain, lead agency planning responsibilities during MOTR execution include:

(1) Leading interagency planning for mission execution.

(2) Planning and coordinating the range of maritime security activities and responses required to execute effective MOTR activities under this plan in order to achieve the USG's desired outcome.

e. **Land and Maritime Commanders. As supported commanders within their AOs, the land and maritime force commanders are responsible for integrating and synchronizing maneuver, fires, and interdiction within their AOs.** Accordingly, land and maritime commanders designate the target priority, effects, and timing of interdiction operations within their AOs. They may designate priority of attacks to focus allocated interdiction assets on the targets or target systems essential to achieving the land or maritime force commanders maneuver objectives. The supported commander specifies desired effects to defeat threats to the maneuver force, to position the enemy for defeat by maneuver forces, and to avoid fratricide or hindrance to friendly maneuver. Timing of operations is synchronized to mass effects at the desired place and time to achieve the objective. Synchronization requires explicit coordination and unity of purpose among the units and components in any operation. Failure to properly coordinate attack of targets within AOs may result in a duplication of effort or increase the risk of fratricide. Maneuver force commanders are assisted in this integration by such elements as the Army's battlefield coordination detachment (BCD) and Marine liaison officer and naval and amphibious liaison element at the JAOC, joint air component coordination element, tactical air control parties, and air liaison officers who provide advice to the maneuver force commander and staff on the capabilities, limitations, and employment of air assets, to include interdiction.

f. Detailed planning facilitates a coherent interdiction effort involving diverse forces using different employment procedures and reduces the potential for fratricide. Interdiction coordination procedures must not inhibit timely application of firepower in the conduct of other operations. Commanders should consider component capabilities for speed, range, maneuver, weapon system characteristics, ability to operate in a potentially contaminated area, IO, intelligence gathering, and ability to receive and distribute information available from space-based assets. Commanders at all levels must ensure interdiction operations are integrated with other ongoing operations. At the joint force level, the joint operations center is the focal point for integrating joint operations at the macro level to include interdiction. Normally, subordinate commanders establish planning cycles for operations based on JFC guidance. This practice permits the coordination of applicable operations, including interdiction, between component commanders early enough and in sufficient detail to allow integration of those operations. Certain time-sensitive targets (TSTs)—highly lucrative, fleeting targets designated by the JFC as high priority—and other targets of opportunity may preclude the use of normal coordination procedures. In such cases, appropriate coordination measures, prior coordination, on-scene command, and ROE should allow rapid attack of these targets. TSTs and other targets of opportunity should be coordinated between affected

> *"For our air offensive to attain its full effect, it is necessary that our ground offensive should be of a character to throw the greatest possible strain upon the enemy's communications."*
>
> **Winston Churchill, 1917**

component commanders prior to attack. When mission objectives, desired effects, and general deconfliction and time sequencing have been jointly planned and integrated at the JAOC for AI operations, details such as attack tactics and individual mission deconfliction can be worked out by those responsible for execution. To ensure a coherent and coordinated effort, a plan for conducting joint interdiction should address two principal areas: a general CONOPS and a description of the planning and coordination cycle required for the phasing of joint interdiction (see Figure III-1).

JOINT INTERDICTION PLAN

The concept of operations should include:

- Identification of objectives and resource requirements necessary to sustain activities
- An orderly schedule of anticipated decisions needed to shape and direct the conduct of joint interdiction
- Phases for related joint interdiction operations
- Arrangements for orchestrating the operations of air, land, maritime, and special operations forces to ensure an integrated effort
- Scheme of support operations needed to assist and protect forces engaged in joint interdiction operations
- Provisions for feedback or analysis concerning the effectiveness of joint interdiction operations

The planning and coordination cycle should:

- Emphasize simplicity
- Emphasize mission-type orders when appropriate
- Ensure availability of appropriate forces and capabilities for employment
- Ensure that component efforts support and reinforce each other to minimize duplication and conflicting actions
- Arrange tasking and coordination of support operations to assist and protect forces engaged in joint interdiction
- Preclude adverse effects on other friendly forces and operations
- Ensure the continuance of effective operations during periods of degraded communications
- Provide flexibility to adapt to changing conditions and priorities

Figure III-1. Joint Interdiction Plan

5. Targeting

The JFC is responsible for all aspects of planning and targeting, from establishing objectives, coordination, and deconfliction between component commanders, to assessment of operations. Targeting is the process of selecting and prioritizing targets and matching the appropriate response to them, taking account of operational requirements and capabilities. Targeting proceeds from the definition of the problem to an assessment of the results achieved by the executed COAs. During target development, the targeting process must relate specific targets to objectives, desired effects, and accompanying actions. Interdiction should focus on those systems that will result in the greatest payoff and achieve the objectives. The targeting process is complicated by the requirement to deconflict duplicative efforts, to prevent fratricide, to ensure compliance with the law of armed conflict (LOAC), to perform collateral damage estimation, and to synchronize and integrate the interdiction of those targets with other activities of the joint force.

a. The goal for interdiction targeting is to execute a connected series of missions and attacks to achieve the JFC's interdiction objectives. A highly effective coordination tool or organization to facilitate this process is the joint targeting coordination board (JTCB). The JTCB is a group formed by the JFC to accomplish broad targeting oversight functions that may include but are not limited to coordinating targeting information, providing targeting guidance and priorities, and refining the joint integrated prioritized target list. The board is normally comprised of representatives from the joint force staff, all components, and if required, component subordinate units.

Additional details on the JTCB and targeting doctrine can be found in JP 3-30, Command and Control for Joint Air Operations, *and JP 3-60,* Joint Targeting.

b. Joint interdiction assets are limited resources. Nominated targets will usually outnumber available assets. A component commander's number one priority may be the JFC's tenth priority (based on the JFC's scheme of maneuver, objectives, or CONOPS for a given period or phase of the campaign). Interdiction operations within AOs occur simultaneously with joint interdiction operations that have a theater/JOA-wide range. Coordination, communication, and feedback between components regarding targeting decisions are essential and enhance trust between supported, supporting, and subordinate commanders and forces. Under most circumstances, the ATO achieves the desired coordination for planned AI missions.

c. Dynamic interdiction missions meet specific requests which arise during an operation, and by their sudden nature are not planned in advance. Dynamic interdiction missions respond to targets that require time sensitive or immediate attention. The same quick-responsive nature of dynamic interdiction that allows it to take advantage of fleeting opportunities can also have a negative impact on individual mission success. Deliberate interdiction requests allow joint interdiction forces more time to study target imagery and to align attack axes to optimize weapons effects. Detailed study can reduce threat exposure and allow mission planners to optimize the weapon's fusing for maximum effect. Deliberate interdiction allows better packaging of interdiction and support assets when required. **The bottom line for dynamic targeting is that it should be used in those cases when the need for a short reaction time outweighs the reduced effectiveness that may result when compared with deliberate operations.** Moreover, opportunity costs must be considered. Commanders should ensure the benefits of diverting interdiction assets away from a planned target outweigh the costs by pondering several variables. Is it affordable to delay striking a planned target? What are the priorities? Will diverting assets to a target of opportunity create greater effects or is it less efficient? In short, the payoff of interdicting a target of opportunity should be worth the cost of diverting planned assets.

Additional information on time-sensitive targeting can be found in the FM 3-60.1, MCRP 3-16D, NTTP 3-60.1, AFTTP(I) 3-2.1, Multi-Service Tactics, Techniques, and Procedures for Targeting Time-Sensitive Targets.

6. Intelligence, Surveillance, and Reconnaissance Strategy and Planning

ISR forces support interdiction planning through the collection of and collaboration on a broad range of information. Commanders require information systems that facilitate exploitation, sharing, and appropriate dissemination of real-time and near real-time intelligence. Planners must ensure that information collection is focused in the most critical areas (collection management) and that the information is analyzed, disseminated, shared, and collaborated into a useful product that supports effective interdiction planning and targeting operations against what is many times, a "fleeting target set."

a. Priority intelligence requirements are developed to support interdiction operations. To that end, joint interdiction targets must be identified and then prioritized to facilitate collection management and mission accomplishment.

Collection management relationships are discussed further in JP 2-01, Joint and National Intelligence Support to Military Operations.

b. **Joint intelligence preparation of the operational environment (JIPOE) is the analytical process used by joint intelligence organizations to produce intelligence assessments, estimates, and other intelligence products in support of the JFC's decision-making process.** JIPOE is a continuous process which enables JFCs and their staffs to visualize the full spectrum of adversary capabilities and potential COAs across all dimensions of the operational environment.

JIPOE is discussed further in JP 2-01.3, Joint Intelligence Preparation of the Operational Environment.

7. Interdiction Planning Considerations

The nature of the mission or a target set may determine its suitability for interdiction and what forces and weapon systems should be employed. For example, a pipeline in the jungle might best be attacked by SOF elements whereas clandestine river transportation of weapons or illegal cargo may best be interdicted by shallow draft boats. The fewer the routes and depots in an enemy transportation system, and the more the enemy depends on that system, the more that system may be vulnerable to interdiction. Conversely, an enemy who possesses a varied, dispersed transportation system is usually much less affected by LOC interdiction. Mobile or easily concealed targets may require an approach different from that employed in attacking fixed emplacements.

a. **Target area environmental considerations include restrictive terrain, time of day, adverse weather, and seasonal and temperature effects.** These conditions may camouflage or conceal targets, reduce visibility, and degrade weapon systems and force capabilities. Terrain features may affect acquisition of the target, requiring specialized weapons and attack tactics. For example, heavily forested emplacements or staging areas may be more suited to SOF direct action missions than laser-guided weapons.

(1) Adverse target weather conditions to include humidity and temperature effects, solar activity, lunar illumination, and passive defense measures such as smoke, may conceal targets, reduce visibility, and degrade weapon systems and overall interdiction capabilities. The rate and extent of enemy maneuver may also be influenced by weather conditions. These, in turn, can provide greater interdiction opportunities (for example, when enemy maneuver is restricted to a few major routes or by seasonal conditions, it results in the concentration of forces). Accurate weather information facilitates the joint force's ability to maximize the performance of its personnel and systems, such as forecasting the electro-optical environment (thermal crossover periods and other TA data) for employing advanced weapon systems. Accurate weather information can increase the probability of successful interdiction and enables friendly forces to exploit weather-induced limitations of enemy forces and systems.

(2) Technology has enhanced detection and identification of obscured targets. For example, night vision devices and electronic sensors can greatly reduce the concealment previously provided by limited visibility. More importantly, assets equipped with advanced sensors, such as JSTARS and UA systems, can direct interdiction assets onto immediate, high-value TSTs which might otherwise be undetectable.

(3) Target defenses may distract or target aircrews, reducing the effectiveness of AI. Detection assets, such as JSTARS and UA or the use of all-source intelligence, may enhance TA. However, enemy air defenses may not allow interdiction aircrew adequate time or avenues to acquire their target visually due to high speeds, low or medium altitudes, or restricted ingress routing necessary to minimize the risk of engagement. Effective force packaging can reduce the impact of enemy air defenses and achieve local air superiority.

b. **Interdiction operations in urban areas can be problematic and require special considerations during planning.** To begin with, collateral damage in cities or towns that have not been evacuated will represent a great risk that must be considered and minimized. One real, alleged, or staged collateral damage or fratricide event can have strategic impact, affecting world opinion, ROE, and host nation restrictions on operations. Planners should integrate public affairs and MISO into interdiction operations from strategy development through mission execution. Next, planners need to account for weather effects caused by the urban environment. Factors include increased pollution and aerosols affecting target detection, warmer temperatures affecting infrared signatures, and variable wind speeds affected by building layout. Finally, urban operations, by their very nature, involve significant LOAC considerations. In particular, commanders must determine the military necessity of an operation, the proportionality of the damage that will be caused, and whether the potential harm to civilians outweighs the importance of the operation. Interdiction forces must give extra attention to the axis of attack and target designation; the problem may be similar to attacking enemy forces in steep mountainous terrain. Larger urban areas with more vertically developed buildings add increased target elevation issues to the targeting problem, and the combination of tall buildings and narrow streets can cause an "urban canyon" effect leading to masking issues for line-of-sight munitions and targeting sensors. Munitions effects will vary greatly depending on whether the enemy can be attacked in the open versus inside buildings, requiring both patience and flexibility for mission success. Planners and operators should take great care in choosing the correct delivery method, munition, and fusing option when employing fires in an urban environment.

For additional information on joint collateral damage procedures, see CJCSI 3160.01, No-Strike and the Collateral Damage Estimation Methodology. *For additional information on collateral damage risk to civilians, civilian structures, and properties associated with CAS attacks, see JP 3-09.3,* Close Air Support.

c. While there are many similarities between air operations over land and sea, important differences exist:

(1) **Maritime rules of engagement.** The maritime environment encompasses historical laws of the sea that impact ROE (e.g., territorial waters versus high seas).

(2) **Maritime airspace control.** Nearly every combatant has a powerful radar sensor/weapons system; as a result, maritime airspace control tends to be more positive vice procedural. This emphasis on positive control involves more controlling agencies within the maritime domain.

d. **Limitations.** Joint forces operate in accordance with applicable ROE, conduct warfare consistent with international laws recognized by the US, and operate within restraints and constraints specified by their commanders. Military objectives are justified by political, military, and legal necessity and achieved through appropriate and disciplined use of forces. **ROE/rules for the use of force are applied by JFCs as a primary means to ensure that operations adhere to the LOAC and USC.** Many factors influence ROE, including national and international law, national command policy, mission, operational environment, commander's intent, and international agreements regulating conduct. ROE always recognize the inherent right of self-defense. **Properly developed ROE must be clear, tailored to the situation, reviewed for legal sufficiency, and included in training.** ROE typically will vary from operation to operation and may change during an operation. DOD forces operating under USCG TACON per *Memorandum of Agreement between the Department of Defense and the Department of Homeland Security for Department of Defense support to the United States Coast Guard for Maritime Homeland Security* operate in accordance with Coast Guard Use of Force Policy. The JFC may prohibit or restrict joint force attacks on specific targets or objects without specific approval based on political considerations, military risk, the LOAC, and ROE. Targeting restrictions fall into two general categories. Items on the no-strike list are those designated by the appropriate authority upon which attacks are prohibited. Restricted targets are legitimate targets that have specific restrictions imposed to avoid interfering with military operations, and any actions that exceed those restrictions are prohibited until coordinated and approved by the establishing headquarters. Targets may have certain restriction caveats associated with them that should be clearly documented in the restricted target list (for example, do not strike during daytime; strike only with a certain weapon, etc.). Some require special precautions (e.g., chemical, biological, or nuclear facilities, proximity to no-strike facilities). Many traditional interdiction targets such as bridges, power generation systems, dams, and other infrastructure may be placed on the restricted list to avoid indiscriminate effects on the civilian population and a lengthy rebuilding process when major combat operations (MCOs) are complete. In addition, structures such as bridges may be vital for use by tactical forces during MCOs; attacking them in this case is counterproductive.

For additional information, see JP 3-60, Joint Targeting.

e. JFCs must consider the potential requirements for interagency coordination as a part of their activities across the range of military operations. **Early inclusion of interagency considerations in assessments, estimates, and plans for military operations will facilitate civil-military integration of effort, focus the appropriate military participation, and assist the military effort to obtain the best available support from other interagency participants. At the same time, DOD must be prepared to support other federal, state, and local agencies as appropriate.** No activity—not major combat against a near peer competitor, interdiction of WMD in international waters, or enforcing sanctions—is totally a military operation. Interagency participants, from the Department of State to the DHS have interest in and requirements to participate in planning military interdiction operations. For example, maritime interdiction/interception actions against a vessel with suspected WMD cargo en route to a US port could easily involve US Navy (DOD), US Coast Guard (DHS), DOS, Central Intelligence Agency, Department of Energy, and Department of Justice activity. Two tools that JFCs and their staffs can use to facilitate interagency coordination are: annex V (Interagency Coordination) to operation plans designed to enhance interagency planning and coordination with partner agencies in carrying out assigned missions; and the joint interagency coordination group.

For more information on interagency activities, see JP 3-08, Interorganizational Coordination During Joint Operations.

f. Today's security environment is extremely fluid, with continually changing coalitions, alliances, partnerships, and new (both national and transnational) threats constantly appearing and disappearing. **Joint forces should be prepared for operations with forces from other nations within the framework of an alliance or coalition.** When conducting interdiction, JFC and staff must consider the inherent complexity of coordinating with multinational partners.

(1) Participation in multinational operations may be complicated by varying national obligations derived from international agreements (i.e., other members in a coalition may not be signatories to treaties that bind the United States, or they may be bound by treaties to which the United States is not a party). **Uneven capabilities of allies and coalition partners complicate the integration of multinational partners and the coordination and synchronization of their activities during multinational operations.**

(2) Alliances typically have compatible C2 structures and weapon systems but many multinational partners will not. This can have a detrimental effect on multinational operations to include interdiction. **As we increasingly digitize the operational environment, we must take into account the capabilities of our multinational partners and the possible limiting effects of their C2 structure.**

(3) Each partner in multinational operations possesses a unique cultural identity—the result of language, values, religion, and economic and social outlooks. Language differences often present the most immediate challenge. **Information lost during translation can be substantial, and miscommunication or misunderstanding can have disastrous effects.**

(4) **An ability to share valuable information helps build trust and confidence, and is beneficial to effective integration of the complex interactions required to succeed in any operations against an enemy. Therefore, it is incumbent on the JFC to develop processes and procedures that facilitate the sharing of information.** In addition, the Commander, Joint Task Force, should consider establishing a civil-military operations center to ensure maximum unity of effort and ease coordination for development of processes and procedures.

8. Joint Interdiction Preparation

a. **Positioning of Interdiction Forces.** Interdiction forces must be positioned in a manner that will allow attack on enemy vulnerabilities. During the earliest stage of planning, JFCs must ensure that the correct mix of interdiction assets will be in place. **Forces should be positioned within operational reach of enemy decisive points to support the JFC's CONOPS and exploit unforeseen opportunities.** Commanders must remain flexible and use every available option to ensure success. For example, a host nation might deny basing and overflight rights to joint aircraft. To circumvent this obstacle, air refueling might be required to support interdiction aircraft, unrestricted multinational interdiction aircraft might be utilized or surface forces may need to maneuver to a position where organic weapons are in range of critical interdiction targets.

b. **Operations Rehearsal.** Preparing for interdiction operations includes **organizing and,** where possible, **training forces to conduct operations throughout the JOA.** When it is not possible to train forces in the theater of employment, as with US-based forces with multiple taskings, maximum use should be made of regularly scheduled and ad-hoc exercise opportunities. Realistic joint training during peacetime will dramatically increase the lethality of the joint force. Staffs should be identified and trained for planning and controlling joint operations. **JFCs and the composition of their staffs should reflect the composition of the joint force to ensure that those responsible for employing joint forces have thorough knowledge of their capabilities and limitations.** The training focus for all forces and the basis for exercise objectives should be the combatant commander's joint mission essential task list.

CHAPTER IV
JOINT INTERDICTION EXECUTION

"I will tell you that a commander without the proper C2 assets commands nothing except a desk. You must have the ability to communicate with the forces under your command. You must have the ability to exchange information with them freely, frequently, and on a global basis."

General Ronald R. Fogleman
Former Chief of Staff, United States Air Force, 1995–1997

1. Command and Control of Joint Interdiction Operations

At the highest level, the JFC is responsible for the execution of theater strategy and operations. The joint operations center is the focal point for integrating joint operations at the macro level to include interdiction. Interdiction of enemy forces and infrastructure is an integral part of a joint campaign or major operation. **Joint interdiction operations require an integrated, flexible, and responsive C2 structure to process interdiction requirements and a dependable, interoperable, and secure communications architecture to exercise control.** The JFC exercises C2 through functional or Service component commanders. Each component may perform interdiction as part of their internal mission, employing their organic C2 assets in accordance with their particular tactics, techniques, and procedures.

a. **The JFC normally delegates the planning and execution of theater/JOA-wide interdiction operations involving joint air assets to the JFACC (if established).** The JFACC directs, coordinates, and deconflicts joint AI operations from an operations center which is normally designated a JAOC. The JAOC is structured to operate as a fully integrated facility. JAOC operations rely on expertise from other component liaisons to coordinate requests or requirements and maintain an up-to-date status of the other component operations. The JFACC staff will normally task and allocate most joint AI operations using host component organic C2 architecture. Reliable, secure communications are required to exchange information among all participants. In joint operations, components provide and operate the C2 systems, which have similar functions at each level of command. The JFACC tasks joint AI assets made available for theater/JOA-wide tasking through the JAOC and appropriate Service component C2 systems to ensure the proper integration of interdiction with the surface scheme of maneuver.

b. **Theater Air Control System (TACS).** The TACS is the Air Force component commander's mechanism for controlling component AI assets. It consists of airborne and ground elements to conduct tailored C2 of AI operations. The structure of the TACS should reflect sensor coverage, component liaison elements, and the communications systems required to provide adequate support. As an organic Air Force system, the TACS remains under OPCON of the commander, Air Force forces (COMAFFOR). The air and space operations center (AOC) is the senior C2 element of the TACS and includes personnel and equipment of necessary disciplines to ensure the effective planning and conduct of component air and space operations. The AOC is designed to expand with augmentation to form the JAOC when the COMAFFOR is designated by the JFC as the JFACC.

c. **Army Air-Ground System (AAGS).** Closely related to, and interconnected with, the TACS is the AAGS. **The AAGS provides for interface between Army and tactical air support agencies of other Services in the planning, evaluating, processing, and coordinating of air support requirements and operations.** Utilizing organic staff members and communications equipment, the AAGS works in conjunction with the TACS to coordinate and integrate both Army component aviation support and Air Force component support with Army ground maneuver. Army airspace C2 elements are at the senior Army echelon and extend down through all tactical command levels to the maneuver brigade. The air defense airspace management/brigade aviation element (ADAM/BAE) cell is located at the brigade combat team. The ADAM/BAE coordinates airspace requirements with higher headquarters as well as joint or multinational forces.

(1) Primary coordination between the TACS and the AAGS starts with the Army's BCD in the JAOC and the air component coordination element liaison at the Army component commander's headquarters. The air support operations center (ASOC) is the next level of Air Force-Army integration. **While the JAOC provides control of air power, the ASOC provides primary control of air power in support of the Army.** Integration then continues down through the Air Force component liaisons aligned with land combat forces. When integrated, the TACS and AAGS are collectively known as the TACS-AAGS (see Figure IV-1).

(2) During linear operations, the ASOC normally controls all airspace short of the FSCL while the JAOC controls airspace beyond the FSCL. ASOC capabilities should be defined and planned for before operations begin. Considerations include, but are not limited to, physical location of the ASOC, terrain, and FSCL depth. AI missions conducted short of the FSCL in an Army force AO, whether or not in support of the Army force, must be coordinated with the ASOC.

d. The **Navy tactical air control system (NTACS)** is the principal air control system afloat. The NTACS is comprised of the United States Navy (USN) tactical air control center (TACC), tactical air direction center, and helicopter direction center. **The TACC is the primary air control agency within the AO from which all air operations supporting the amphibious task force are controlled.**

e. **Marine Air Command and Control System (MACCS).** The MACCS consists of various air C2 agencies designed to provide the Marine air-ground task force aviation combat element commander with the ability to monitor, supervise, and influence the application of Marine and supporting air assets. Marine aviation's philosophy is one of centralized control and decentralized execution. The Marine force's focal point for tasking and exercising OPCON over Marine Corps air forces is the tactical air command center, which performs similar duties for organic Marine aviation that the JAOC performs for joint air component operations. The direct air support center (DASC) is roughly equivalent to the Air Force's ASOC.

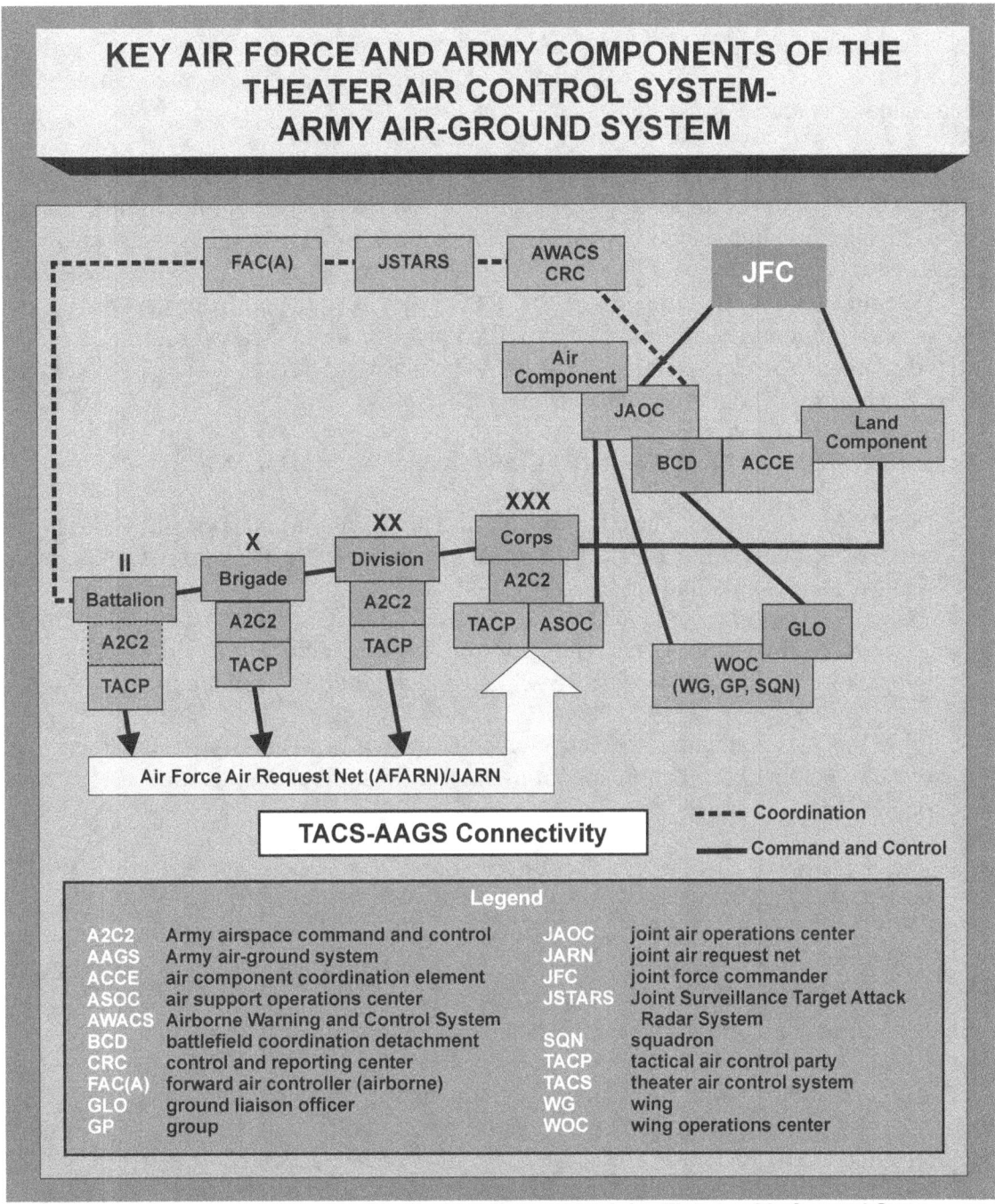

KEY AIR FORCE AND ARMY COMPONENTS OF THE THEATER AIR CONTROL SYSTEM-ARMY AIR-GROUND SYSTEM

Legend

A2C2	Army airspace command and control	JAOC	joint air operations center
AAGS	Army air-ground system	JARN	joint air request net
ACCE	air component coordination element	JFC	joint force commander
ASOC	air support operations center	JSTARS	Joint Surveillance Target Attack Radar System
AWACS	Airborne Warning and Control System		
BCD	battlefield coordination detachment	SQN	squadron
CRC	control and reporting center	TACP	tactical air control party
FAC(A)	forward air controller (airborne)	TACS	theater air control system
GLO	ground liaison officer	WG	wing
GP	group	WOC	wing operations center

Figure IV-1. Key Air Force and Army Components of the Theater Air Control System-Army Air-Ground System

f. **Special Operations.** Theater special operations are normally under the control of the joint force special operations component commander (JFSOCC). If designated by the JFSOCC, control of SOF airpower is normally exercised by a joint special operations air component commander (JSOACC). If a JSOACC has not been designated, then SOF airpower is controlled by its Service component within the joint force special operations command. The JFSOCC provides a special operations liaison element (SOLE) to the JFACC. The SOLE director reports directly to the JFSOCC and does not have operational control of any SOF assets. The role of the SOLE is to coordinate, deconflict, and integrate special operations air, surface, and subsurface operations with conventional air operations. The SOLE can provide timely operational environment awareness which can enhance interdiction operations.

g. **Theater Air-Ground System (TAGS).** The digitalization of the modern operational environment has improved the JFACC's ability to command and control joint interdiction airpower. The speed and nonlinear aspects of modern warfare, as well as the precision of today's weapons, dictate close coordination on the AO among the JFC's components. **The JFACC must ensure all elements of the TAGS are in place and the various liaison positions throughout the command chain filled prior to, or as soon as possible after, the start of an operation or campaign.** When all elements of the TACS, AAGS, MACCS, and NTACS integrate, the entire system is labeled the TAGS.

h. Joint Automated Deep Operations Coordination System (JADOCS)

(1) JADOCS facilitates the integration of joint/multinational fires. Digital integration of US and multinational fires systems enables timely execution of TSTs, high-payoff targets, and high-value targets.

(2) The joint management function provides the ability to rapidly change and display operational graphics and FSCMs while conducting joint fire support.

(3) The AI planning and execution function provides more effective employment of AI assets through timely and improved information flow for the identification, assignment, and nomination of AI targets.

For more information on JADOCS, see JP 3-09, Joint Fire Support.

i. Navy and Coast Guard forces may have specific targets for interdiction or they may operate in patrol areas. The distances involved and the ambiguity of possible threats at sea require operational flexibility. C2 may be through a task force, other military chain of command, or in some instances of MOTR plan execution, directly through national level authorities. Both USN and USCG may respond under Title 10, USC, authority. However, unless the situation involves a major and immediate threat requiring emergency USN response as the only/most capable available force, USCG will respond if mission requirements dictate, under Title 14, USC, law enforcement authority.

j. Within the maritime domain, authority for control of AI of maritime target assets is derived from the JFMCC as the supported commander. The JFACC may allocate sorties, via the ATO, to provide reconnaissance and surveillance—often referred to as surface surveillance coordination—and AI in the maritime AO. These sorties play a critical role in targeting and establishing/maintaining a common operational picture. In most cases, the sea combat commander or the SUWC will be authorized to designate surface contacts for strike during AI of maritime target execution.

2. Operational Area Geometry and Coordination

a. **JFCs may employ various control and coordinating measures to facilitate effective joint operations.** These measures may include establishing boundaries, objectives, coordinating altitudes to deconflict air operations, air defense areas, amphibious objective areas, and submarine operating areas. Boundaries require special emphasis because of their implications on the integration of interdiction and maneuver. **Boundaries define areas in order to facilitate integration and deconfliction of operations.** In land and maritime operations, a boundary is a line that defines areas between adjacent units or formations. A boundary may be designated for maritime operations adjacent to the area of land conflict to enhance coordination and execution of maritime operations. Integration of efforts and synchronization of activities within the land or maritime operational boundaries is particularly important.

(1) The JFC may use lateral, rear, and forward boundaries to define AOs for land and maritime forces. These are sized, shaped, and positioned to enable land or maritime forces to accomplish their mission while protecting forces. Theater air sorties are not constrained by land boundaries, per se. However, since the airspace above surface areas is used by all components of the joint force, JFCs promulgate airspace control measures to deconflict the necessary multiple uses required (see JP 3-52, *Joint Airspace Control*).

(2) Boundaries are based on the JFC's CONOPS and the land or naval force commander's requirement for depth to maneuver rapidly and to fight at extended ranges.

b. **Operational Environment Geometry. Joint interdiction may be conducted in conjunction with friendly forces operating in an AO.** In order to integrate joint fires and avoid fratricide, FSCMs must be established. When air operations are involved, airspace coordinating measures will normally be used along with FSCMs. Before discussing coordinating measures, a brief background on operational environment geometry will provide a better understanding for the types of FSCMs required in interdiction operations.

(1) Operational areas may be contiguous or noncontiguous (see Figure IV-2). When they are contiguous, a boundary separates them. When operational areas are noncontiguous, they do not share a boundary; the CONOPS links the elements of the force. A noncontiguous operational area normally is characterized by a 360-degree boundary. The higher headquarters is responsible for the area between noncontiguous operational areas (JP 3-0, *Joint Operations*).

(2) Operations may be linear or nonlinear in nature (see Figure IV-3). In linear operations, commanders direct and sustain combat power toward enemy forces in concert with adjacent units. Linear perspective refers primarily to the conduct of operations along lines of operations with identified forward lines of own troops (FLOTs). In linear operations, emphasis is placed on maintaining the position of the land force in relation to other friendly forces. This positioning usually results in contiguous operations where surface forces share boundaries. Linear operations are normally conducted against a deeply arrayed, echeloned enemy force or when the threat to LOCs requires control of the terrain around those LOCs. In these circumstances, linear operations allow commanders to concentrate and

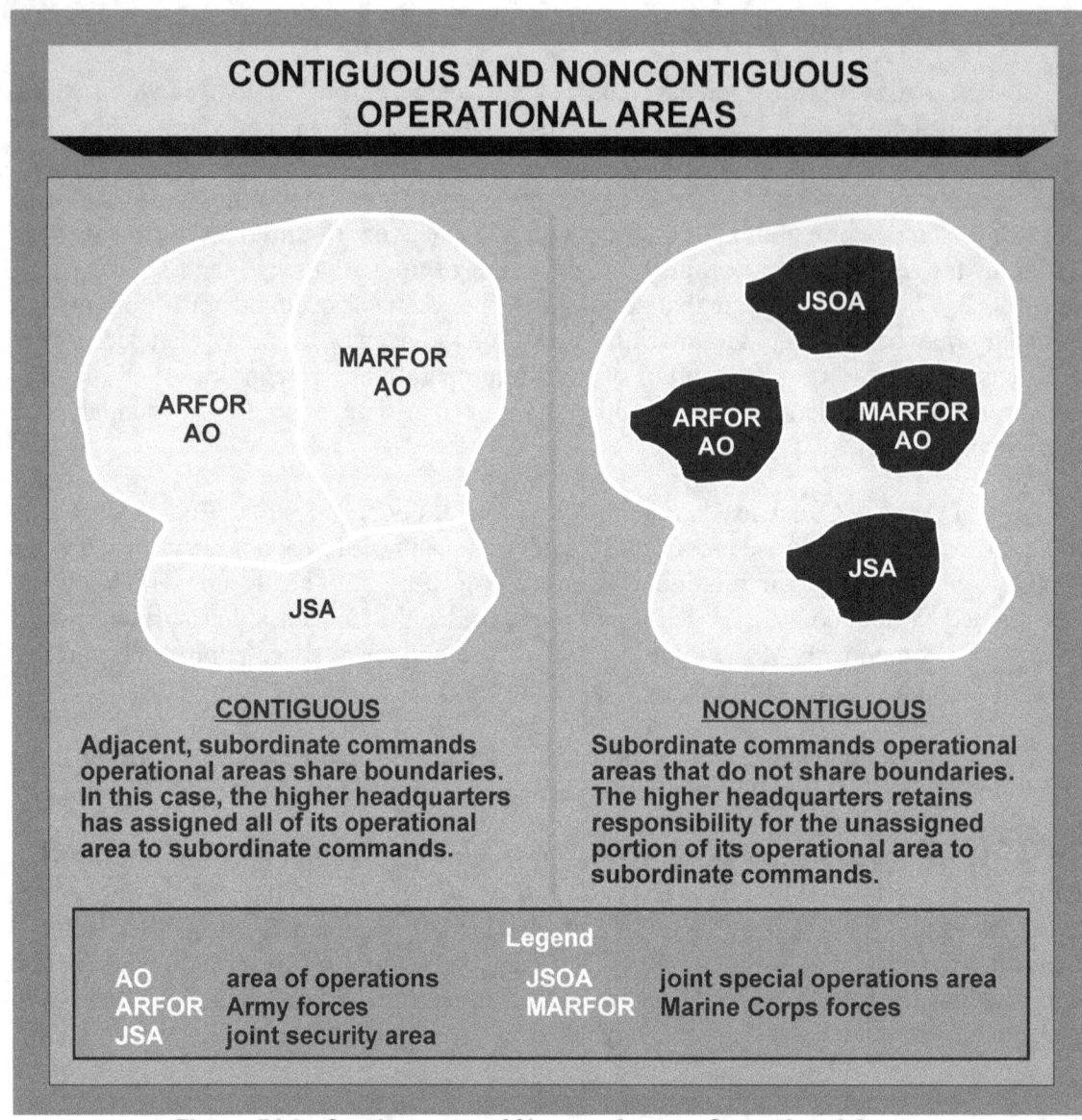

CONTIGUOUS AND NONCONTIGUOUS OPERATIONAL AREAS

CONTIGUOUS

Adjacent, subordinate commands operational areas share boundaries. In this case, the higher headquarters has assigned all of its operational area to subordinate commands.

NONCONTIGUOUS

Subordinate commands operational areas that do not share boundaries. The higher headquarters retains responsibility for the unassigned portion of its operational area to subordinate commands.

Legend

AO	area of operations	JSOA	joint special operations area
ARFOR	Army forces	MARFOR	Marine Corps forces
JSA	joint security area		

Figure IV-2. Contiguous and Noncontiguous Operational Areas

integrate combat power more easily. World War I, World War II, and the Korean War offer multiple examples of linear operations while more recent examples include maneuver during Operation DESERT STORM and the drive to Baghdad during OIF.

(3) **In nonlinear operations, forces orient on objectives without geographic reference to adjacent forces.** Nonlinear operations are usually characterized by noncontiguous operations. Nonlinear operations emphasize simultaneous operations along multiple lines of operation from selected bases. Nonlinear operations place a premium on intelligence, mobility, and sustainment. OEF is an excellent example of nonlinear operations. Joint forces orient more on their assigned objectives (for example, destroying an enemy force or seizing and controlling critical terrain or population centers) and less on their geographic relationship to other friendly forces.

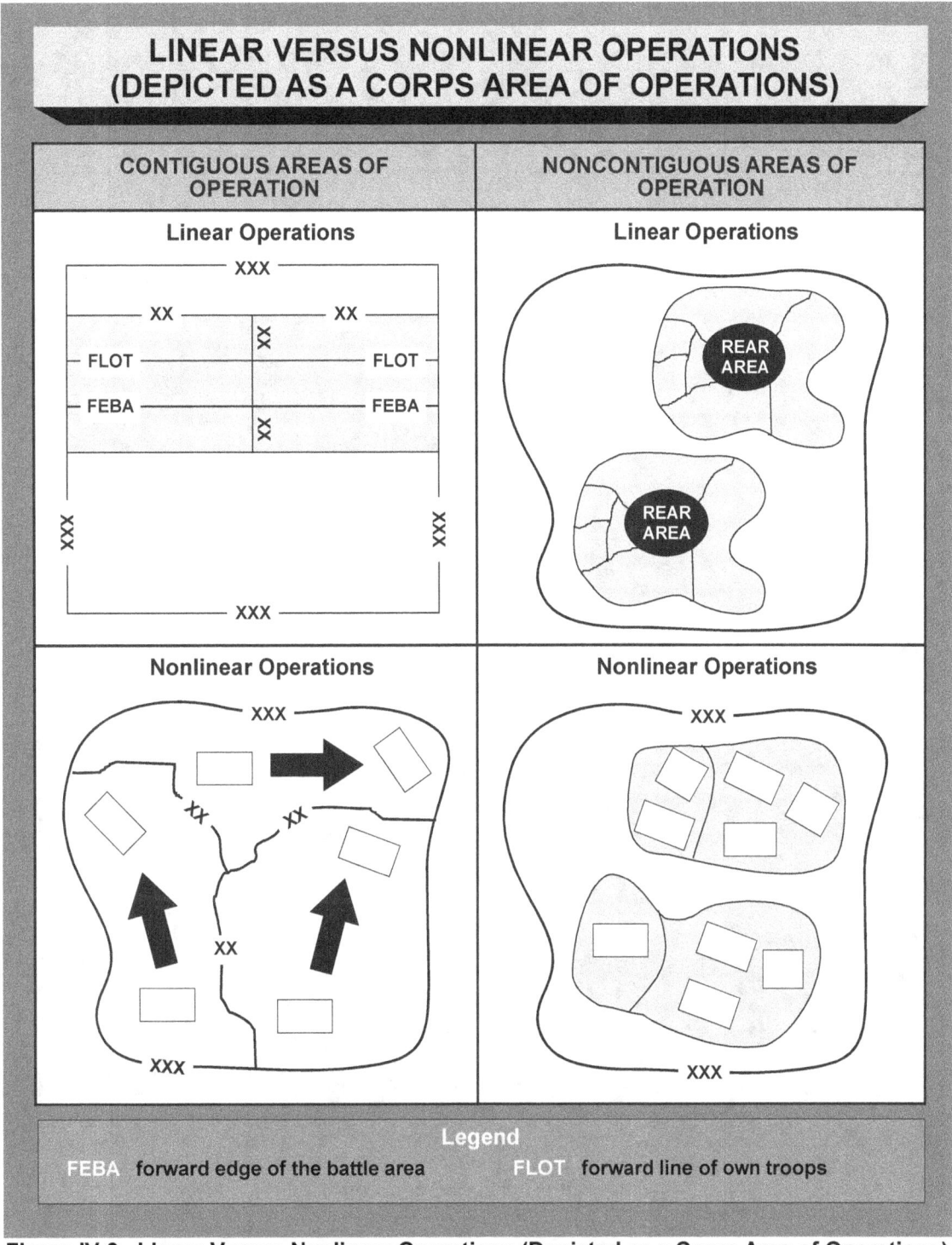

Figure IV-3. Linear Versus Nonlinear Operations (Depicted as a Corps Area of Operations)

For additional information on nonlinear operations, see JP 3-0, Joint Operations.

3. Coordinating Measures

a. There are two important constructs to understand when discussing coordinating measures (see Figure IV-4).

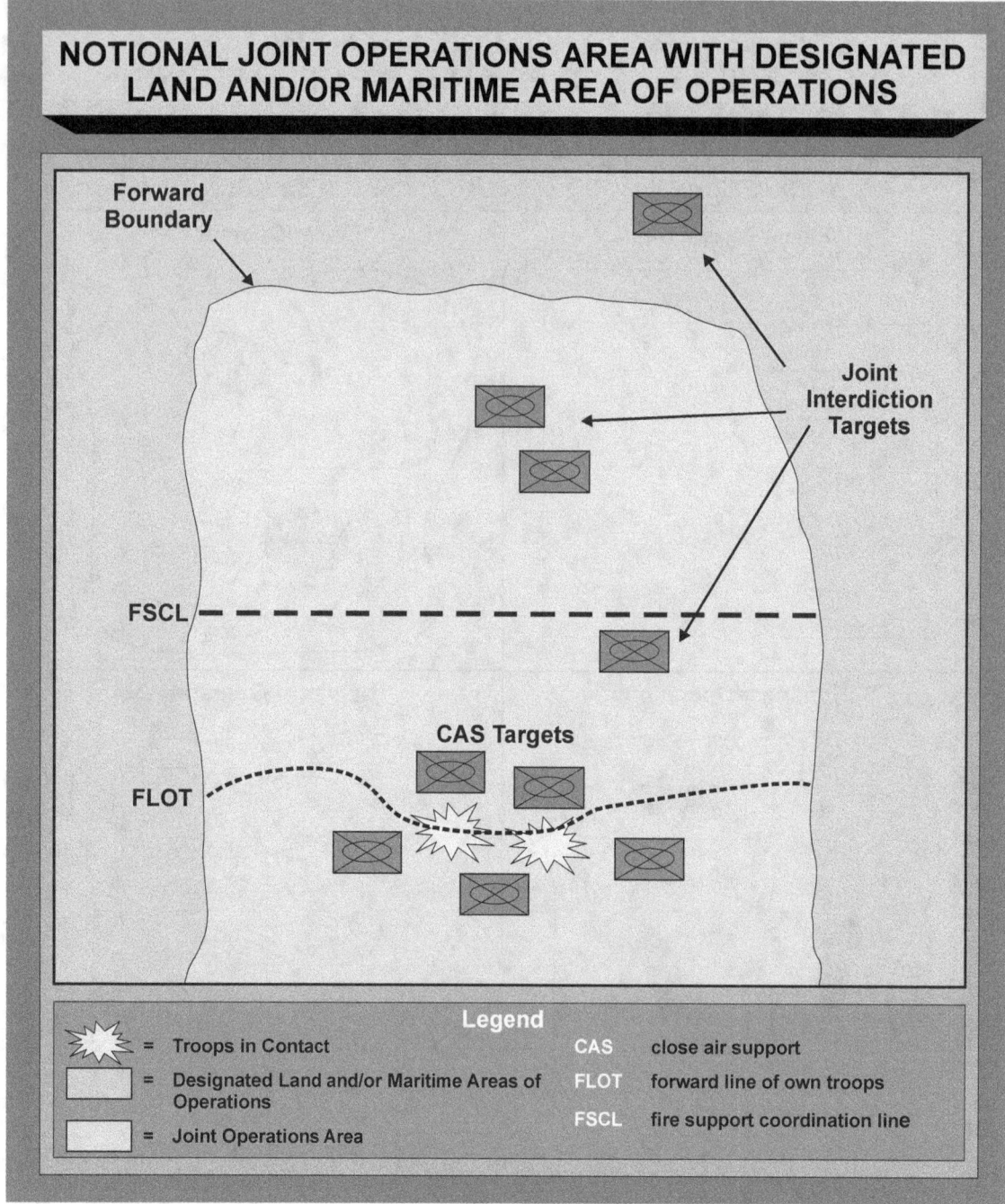

Figure IV-4. Notional Joint Operations Area with Designated Land and/or Maritime Area of Operations

(1) The forward boundary (FB) defines a component's outer AO and is the farthest limit of an organization's responsibility. The organization is responsible for deep operations to that limit. Within the JOA, the next higher headquarters is responsible for coordinating deep operations beyond the FB. In offensive operations, the FB may move from phase line to phase line, depending on the AO situation.

(2) The FLOT is a line that indicates the most forward positions of friendly forces during linear operations at a specific time. The FLOT normally includes the forward location of covering and screening forces. The zone between the FLOT and the FSCL is typically the area over which friendly ground forces intend to maneuver in the near future and is also the area where joint AI operations are normally executed through the ASOC/DASC.

b. **FSCM.** Within their AOs, land and naval force commanders employ permissive and restrictive FSCMs. **FSCMs are necessary to facilitate the rapid engagement of targets and simultaneously provide safeguards for friendly forces. Permissive FSCMs facilitate attacks and include coordinated fire lines, free fire areas, FSCLs, and kill boxes. Restrictive measures safeguard friendly forces and include no-fire areas, restrictive fire areas, restrictive fire lines, and airspace coordination areas.**

(1) The FSCL is a significant consideration during interdiction operations. When appropriate, an FSCL will be established and adjusted by appropriate land or amphibious force commanders within their assigned boundaries in consultation with superior, subordinate, supporting, and affected commanders. The purpose of the FSCL is to facilitate the expeditious attack of surface targets of opportunity beyond the coordinating measure. The FSCL applies to all fires of air, land, and sea-based weapon systems using any type of ammunition against surface targets. The FSCL does not divide an AO by defining a boundary between close and deep operations or a zone for CAS.

(2) The FSCL is primarily used to establish C2 procedures for planning and execution purposes—it does not define mission types. Interdiction can occur both short of and beyond the FSCL. Attacks on surface targets short of the FSCL during the conduct of joint interdiction operations must be controlled by and/or coordinated with the appropriate land or amphibious force commander. While conducting AI short of the FSCL, mission updates through a TACS or amphibious TACS agency can help ensure that those targets are still valid, eliminate redundant targeting, and reduce the potential for fratricide. An example of this type of coordinating agency is an ASOC, DASC, or TACC.

(a) Interdiction of targets short of the FSCL is controlled by the appropriate land or amphibious force commander. Coordination is normally conducted through such agencies as the Army fires cell and fire support coordination center. This coordination is facilitated by C2 platforms or centers such as JSTARS, BCD, ASOC, DASC, TACC, or SOLE.

(b) Joint interdiction forces attacking targets beyond the FSCL must inform all affected commanders in sufficient time to allow necessary reaction to avoid friendly casualties. SOF operations beyond the FSCL and outside the land force AO are particularly at risk and require detailed coordination. In exceptional circumstances, the inability to inform affected commanders will not preclude the attack of targets beyond the FSCL. However, failure to coordinate this type of attack increases the risk of fratricide and could waste limited and hard to replace resources.

(c) The decision on where to place (or even to use) an FSCL requires careful consideration. Placement of the FSCL should strike a balance so as not to unduly inhibit operational tempo while maximizing the effectiveness of organic and joint force interdiction assets. **The optimum placement of the FSCL varies with specific AO circumstances, but considerations include the ground force positions and anticipated scheme of maneuver during the effective time period of the FSCL and their indirect fire support systems' range limits where typically the preponderance of lethal effects on the AO shifts from the ground component to the air component.** In this way, the FSCL placement maximizes the overall effectiveness of the joint force, and each component will suffer only a small reduction in efficiency. The proper location for the FSCL may also shift from one phase of the war operation (or campaign) to the next, depending on the scale and scope of each component's contribution during that phase.

See JP 3-09, Joint Fire Support, *for further discussion of the FSCL.*

   c. **Kill Boxes**

      (1) **Definition.** A kill box is a three-dimensional area used to facilitate the integration of joint fires.

      (2) **Purpose.** When established, the primary purpose of a kill box is to allow lethal attack against surface targets without further coordination with the establishing commander and without terminal attack control. When used to integrate air-to-surface and surface-to-surface indirect fires, the kill box will have appropriate restrictions. The goal is to reduce the coordination required to fulfill support requirements with maximum flexibility, while preventing fratricide.

      (3) **Establishment.** A kill box is established and adjusted by supported component commanders in consultation with superior, subordinate, supporting, and affected commanders, and is an extension of an existing support relationship established by the JFC.

See FM 3-09.34/MCRP 3-25H/NTTP 3-09.2.1/AFTTP(I) 3-2.59, Multi-Service Tactics, Techniques, and Procedures for Kill Box Employment, *for further information.*

4. **Assessment**

   a. Assessment is used to measure progress of the joint force toward mission accomplishment. **Commanders continuously assess the operational environment and the progress of operations, and compare them to their initial vision and intent.** Commanders adjust operations based on their assessment to ensure objectives are met and the desired end state is achieved.

   b. At the tactical level, combat assessment typically focuses on task accomplishment and target engagement. Joint interdiction operations should include both pre- and post-interdiction target reconnaissance efforts in order to facilitate combat assessment. **When combat assessment is linked to current and reliable intelligence, the JFC can accurately assess what was accomplished, the overall effect on the enemy and whether or not the**

enemy has accomplished system reconstitution or an effective workaround solution. Information gained from combat assessment provides input for follow-on interdiction efforts.

For a more in depth explanation of the assessment process, see JP 3-60, Joint Targeting, *Appendix C,* The Assessment Process.

Intentionally Blank

APPENDIX A
REFERENCES

The development of JP 3-03 is based upon the following primary references.

1. General

    a. NSPD-17/HSPD-4, *National Strategy to Combat Weapons of Mass Destruction.*

    b. NSPD-41/HSPD-13, *Maritime Security Policy.*

    c. *Memorandum of Agreement between the Department of Defense and the Department of Homeland Security for Department of Defense support to the United States Coast Guard for Maritime Homeland Security.*

2. Department of Defense

    a. Department of Defense Directive (DODD) 5100.1, *Functions of the Department of Defense and Its Major Components.*

    b. DODD 1400.31, *DOD Civilian Work Force Contingency and Emergency Planning and Execution.*

3. Chairman of the Joint Chiefs of Staff

    a. CJCSI 3520.02A, *Proliferation Security Initiative (PSI) Activity Program.*

    b. CJCSI 5120.02B, *Joint Doctrine Development System.*

    c. JP 1, *Doctrine for the Armed Forces of the United States.*

    d. JP 1-02, *DOD Dictionary of Military and Associated Terms.*

    e. JP 2-0, *Joint Intelligence.*

    f. JP 2-01, *Joint and National Intelligence Support to Military Operations.*

    g. JP 3-0, *Joint Operations.*

    h. JP 3-01, *Countering Air and Missile Threats.*

    i. JP 3-02, *Amphibious Operations.*

    j. JP 3-05, *Special Operations.*

    k. JP 3-05.1, *Joint Special Operations Task Force Operations.*

    l. JP 3-09, *Joint Fire Support.*

m. JP 3-13, *Information Operations.*

n. JP 3-13.1, *Electronic Warfare.*

o. JP 3-14, *Space Operations.*

p. JP 3-15, *Barriers, Obstacles, and Mine Warfare for Joint Operations.*

q. JP 3-18, *Forcible Entry Operations.*

r. JP 3-30, *Command and Control for Joint Air Operations.*

s. JP 3-40, *Combating Weapons of Mass Destruction.*

t. JP 3-52, *Joint Airspace Control.*

u. JP 3-60, *Joint Targeting.*

v. JP 3-61, *Public Affairs.*

w. JP 4-0, *Joint Logistics.*

x. JP 5-0, *Joint Operation Planning.*

y. JP 6-0, *Joint Communications System.*

APPENDIX B
ADMINISTRATIVE INSTRUCTIONS

1. User Comments

Users in the field are highly encouraged to submit comments on this publication to: Joint Staff J-7, Deputy Director, Joint and Coalition Warfighting, Joint and Coalition Warfighting Center, ATTN: Joint Doctrine Support Division, 116 Lake View Parkway, Suffolk, VA 23435-2697. These comments should address content (accuracy, usefulness, consistency, and organization), writing, and appearance.

2. Authorship

The lead agent for this publication is the US Air Force. The Joint Staff doctrine sponsor for this publication is the operations directorate of a joint staff.

3. Supersession

This publication supersedes JP 3-03, 03 May 2007, *Joint Interdiction.*

4. Change Recommendations

a. Recommendations for urgent changes to this publication should be submitted:

TO: JOINT STAFF WASHINGTON DC//J7-JEDD//

b. Routine changes should be submitted electronically to the Deputy Director, Joint and Coalition Warfighting, Joint and Coalition Warfighting Center, Joint Doctrine Support Division and info the lead agent and the Director for Joint Force Development, J-7/JEDD.

c. When a Joint Staff directorate submits a proposal to the CJCS that would change source document information reflected in this publication, that directorate will include a proposed change to this publication as an enclosure to its proposal. The Services and other organizations are requested to notify the Joint Staff J-7 when changes to source documents reflected in this publication are initiated.

5. Distribution of Publications

Local reproduction is authorized and access to unclassified publications is unrestricted. However, access to and reproduction authorization for classified joint publications must be in accordance with DOD 5200.1-R, *Information Security Program.*

6. Distribution of Electronic Publications

a. Joint Staff J-7 will not print copies of JPs for distribution. Electronic versions are available on JDEIS at https://jdeis.js.mil (NIPRNET) and http://jdeis.js.smil.mil (SIPRNET), and on the JEL at http://www.dtic.mil/doctrine (NIPRNET).

b. Only approved JPs and joint test publications are releasable outside the CCMDs, Services, and Joint Staff. Release of any classified JP to foreign governments or foreign nationals must be requested through the local embassy (Defense Attaché Office) to DIA, Defense Foreign Liaison/IE-3, 200 MacDill Blvd., Joint Base Anacostia-Bolling, Washington, DC 20340-5100.

c. JEL CD-ROM. Upon request of a joint doctrine development community member, the Joint Staff J-7 will produce and deliver one CD-ROM with current JPs. This JEL CD-ROM will be updated not less than semi-annually and when received can be locally reproduced for use within the combatant commands and Services.

GLOSSARY
PART I—ABBREVIATIONS AND ACRONYMS

AAGS	Army air-ground system
ADAM/BAE	air defense airspace management/brigade aviation element
AFTTP(I)	Air Force tactics, techniques, and procedures (instruction)
AI	air interdiction
AO	area of operations
AOC	air and space operations center (USAF)
ASOC	air support operations center
ATACMS	Army Tactical Missile System
ATO	air tasking order
BCD	battlefield coordination detachment
BDA	battle damage assessment
C2	command and control
CALCM	conventional air-launched cruise missile
COMAFFOR	commander, Air Force forces
CAS	close air support
CJCSI	Chairman of the Joint Chiefs of Staff instruction
COA	course of action
COG	center of gravity
CONOPS	concept of operations
DASC	direct air support center
DHS	Department of Homeland Security
DOD	Department of Defense
DODD	Department of Defense directive
EMIO	expanded maritime interception operations
EW	electronic warfare
FAC(A)	forward air controller (airborne)
FB	forward boundary
FLOT	forward line of own troops
FM	field manual (Army)
FSCL	fire support coordination line
FSCM	fire support coordination measure
HSPD	homeland security Presidential directive
IO	information operations
ISR	intelligence, surveillance, and reconnaissance

JADOCS	Joint Automated Deep Operations Coordination System
JAOC	joint air operations center
JFACC	joint force air component commander
JFC	joint force commander
JFLCC	joint force land component commander
JFMCC	joint force maritime component commander
JFSOCC	joint force special operations component commander
JIPOE	joint intelligence preparation of the operational environment
JOA	joint operations area
JP	joint publication
JSOACC	joint special operations air component commander
JSTARS	Joint Surveillance Target Attack Radar System
JTCB	joint targeting coordination board
LEDET	law enforcement detachment (USCG)
LEO	law enforcement operations
LOAC	law of armed conflict
LOC	line of communications
MACCS	Marine air command and control system
MAS	maritime air support
MCO	major combat operation
MCRP	Marine Corps reference publication
MDA	maritime domain awareness
MIO	maritime interception operations
MISO	military information support operations
MLRS	multiple launch rocket system
MOTR	maritime operational threat response
NSPD	national security Presidential directive
NTACS	Navy tactical air control system
NTTP	Navy tactics, techniques, and procedures
OEF	Operation ENDURING FREEDOM
OGA	other government agency
OIF	Operation IRAQI FREEDOM
OPCON	operational control
PGM	precision-guided munition
ROE	rules of engagement
SCAR	strike coordination and reconnaissance
SOF	special operations forces
SOLE	special operations liaison element

SR	special reconnaissance
SUWC	surface warfare commander
TA	target acquisition
TACC	tactical air control center (USN)
TACON	tactical control
TACS	theater air control system
TAGS	theater air-ground system
TGO	terminal guidance operations
TLAM	Tomahawk land attack missile
TST	time-sensitive target
UA	unmanned aircraft
USC	United States Code
USCG	United States Coast Guard
USG	United States Government
USN	United States Navy
WMD	weapons of mass destruction

PART II—TERMS AND DEFINITIONS

air interdiction. Air operations conducted to divert, disrupt, delay, or destroy the enemy's military surface capabilities before it can be brought to bear effectively against friendly forces, or to otherwise achieve objectives that are conducted at such distances from friendly forces that detailed integration of each air mission with the fire and movement of friendly forces is not required. (Approved for incorporation into JP 1-02.)

axis of advance. A line of advance assigned for purposes of control; often a road or a group of roads, or a designated series of locations, extending in the direction of the enemy. (Approved for incorporation into JP 1-02 with JP 3-03 as the source JP.)

battlefield coordination detachment. An Army liaison located in the air operations center that provides selected operational functions between the Army forces and the air component commander. Also called **BCD.** (Approved for incorporation into JP 1-02.)

command center. None (Approved for removal from JP 1-02.)

diversion. 1. The act of drawing the attention and forces of an enemy from the point of the principal operation; an attack, alarm, or feint that diverts attention. 2. A change made in a prescribed route for operational or tactical reasons that does not constitute a change of destination. 3. A rerouting of cargo or passengers to a new transshipment point or destination or on a different mode of transportation prior to arrival at ultimate destination. 4. In naval mine warfare, a route or channel bypassing a dangerous area by connecting one channel to another or it may branch from a channel and rejoin it on the other side of the danger. (Approved for incorporation into JP 1-02.)

forward line of own troops. A line that indicates the most forward positions of friendly forces in any kind of military operation at a specific time. Also called **FLOT.** (Approved for incorporation into JP 1-02.)

interdiction. 1. An action to divert, disrupt, delay, or destroy the enemy's military surface capability before it can be used effectively against friendly forces, or to otherwise achieve objectives. 2. In support of law enforcement, activities conducted to divert, disrupt, delay, intercept, board, detain, or destroy, under lawful authority, vessels, vehicles, aircraft, people, cargo, and money. (Approved for incorporation into JP 1-02.)

maritime interception operations. Efforts to monitor, query, and board merchant vessels in international waters to enforce sanctions against other nations such as those in support of United Nations Security Council Resolutions and/or prevent the transport of restricted goods. Also called **MIO.** (Approved for incorporation into JP 1-02 with JP 3-03 as the source JP.)

poststrike reconnaissance. None. (Approved for removal from from JP 1-02.)

precision-guided munition. A guided weapon intended to destroy a point target and minimize collateral damage. Also called **PGM, smart weapon, smart munition.** (Approved for incorporation into JP 1-02.)

strike coordination and reconnaissance. A mission flown for the purpose of detecting targets and coordinating or performing attack or reconnaissance on those targets. Also called **SCAR.** (Approved for incorporation into JP 1-02.)

tactical air support. None. (Approved for removal from JP 1-02.)

tactical diversion. None. (Approved form removal from JP 1-02.)

terminal guidance. 1. The guidance applied to a guided missile between midcourse guidance and arrival in the vicinity of the target. 2. Electronic, mechanical, visual, or other assistance given an aircraft pilot to facilitate arrival at, operation within or over, landing upon, or departure from an air landing or airdrop facility. (JP 1-02. SOURCE: JP 3-03.)

time of attack. None. (Approved for removal from JP 1-02.)

use of force policy. Policy guidance issued by the Commandant, US Coast Guard, on the use of force and weapons. (Approved for incorporation into JP 1-02 with JP 3-03 as the source JP.)

Intentionally Blank

JOINT DOCTRINE PUBLICATIONS HIERARCHY

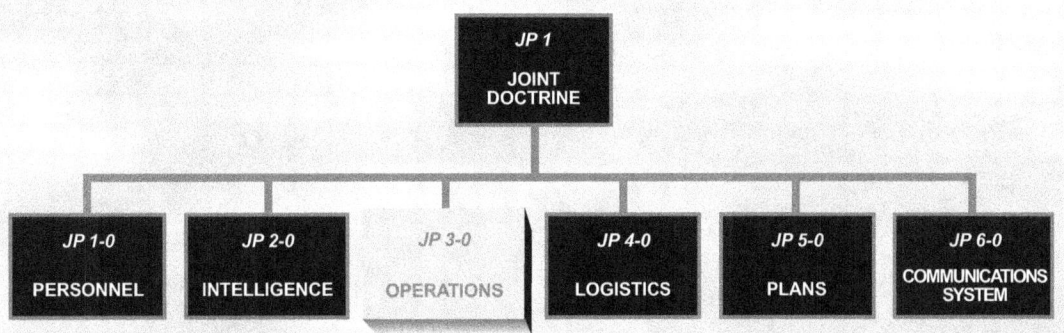

All joint publications are organized into a comprehensive hierarchy as shown in the chart above. **Joint Publication (JP) 3-03** is in the **Operations** series of joint doctrine publications. The diagram below illustrates an overview of the development process:

STEP #4 - Maintenance

- JP published and continuously assessed by users
- Formal assessment begins 24 27 months following publication
- Revision begins 3.5 years after publication
- Each JP revision is completed no later than 5 years after signature

STEP #1 - Initiation

- Joint doctrine development community (JDDC) submission to fill extant operational void
- Joint Staff (JS) J 7 conducts front end analysis
- Joint Doctrine Planning Conference validation
- Program directive (PD) development and staffing/joint working group
- PD includes scope, references, outline, milestones, and draft authorship
- JS J 7 approves and releases PD to lead agent (LA) (Service, combatant command, JS directorate)

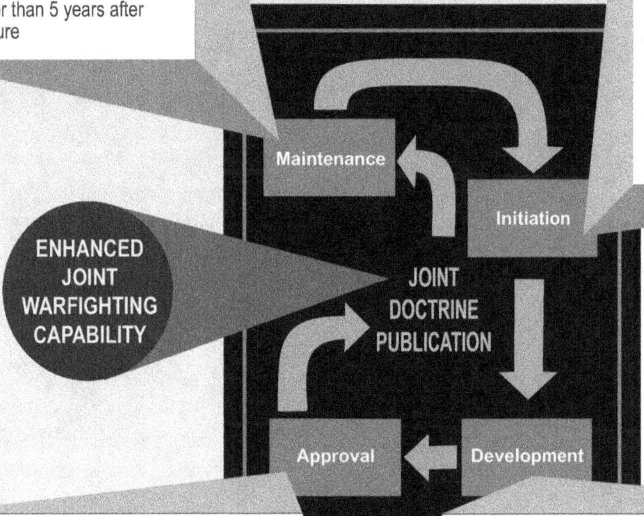

ENHANCED JOINT WARFIGHTING CAPABILITY

Maintenance

Initiation

JOINT DOCTRINE PUBLICATION

Approval

Development

STEP #3 - Approval

- JSDS delivers adjudicated matrix to JS J 7
- JS J 7 prepares publication for signature
- JSDS prepares JS staffing package
- JSDS staffs the publication via JSAP for signature

STEP #2 - Development

- LA selects primary review authority (PRA) to develop the first draft (FD)
- PRA develops FD for staffing with JDDC
- FD comment matrix adjudication
- JS J 7 produces the final coordination (FC) draft, staffs to JDDC and JS via Joint Staff Action Processing (JSAP) system
- Joint Staff doctrine sponsor (JSDS) adjudicates FC comment matrix
- FC joint working group